W9-BVU-563

Madison's
"Advice To My Country"

THE WHIG-CLIO BICENTENNIAL LECTURES

Madison's "Advice To My Country"

By Adrienne Koch

Princeton, New Jersey
Princeton University Press
1966

Library of Congress Catalog Card: 66-12878
Printed in the United States of America
by Quinn & Boden Company, Inc.

To Nancy and Michael

Preface

I Welcome the opportunity given me to participate in the celebration of the Bicentennial of the American Whig–Clio Society. From 1765 to 1965: think of it, a feat of unparalleled survival, dipping back into the years when the movement for American Independence was in its infancy and reaching to a flourishing 1965 and future on the Princeton campus.

Reflecting on the Society's history, I am clearly an outsider. I understand that only one woman, Mrs. Annis Boudinot Stockton, ever "belonged" to the Whigs and that the official reason she was given this honor was that she had gone to great trouble to save the university's property from destruction during the Revolutionary War. I understand that a second version of this affair is that she was chased by a bull, and took hasty refuge inside Nassau Hall. Once she had gained entrance within this male sanctum, she was made a member of the Society, to save appearances. I can imagine a third version, born of today—that she was carefully and expressly chosen from among a corps of friendly ladies in and around Princeton as a "token" pledge that the Whigs were true liberals, freed of prejudice —even of discrimination on grounds of sex! In any event, it was some variety of enlightenment and folly, or both, that prompted the Society to invite me here. Whatever the cause, I cannot help but enjoy the occasion.

Really I am here because of the company I keep. For many years I have been an admirer of one of Whig–Clio's founding fathers, once called by a contemporary "a remarkable sweet man," and by another, "the great little Mr. Madison." Fifteen years ago I published a book called *Jefferson and Madison,* thus making no bones about the fact that Madison himself knew how to choose *his* company. I have always liked a description by Paul Jennings, Madison's mulatto personal servant who later purchased his freedom of Dolley Madison when she lived in Washington after her husband's death. Jennings dictated his "Reminiscences," which were subsequently printed. In them he said:

> While Mr. Jefferson was President, he and Mr. Madison (then his Secretary of State)

> were extremely intimate; in fact, two brothers could not have been more so. Mr. Jefferson always stopped overnight at Mr. Madison's, in going and returning from Washington.[1]

Going and coming from Washington—nostalgically one thinks of that!

My interest in James Madison is not of yesterday's vintage. It goes back to the commencement of my life in scholarship, when I wrote my first book on Thomas Jefferson, a doctoral dissertation written at Columbia University under the guidance of a true master, Herbert Schneider, and published in 1944. Since that time it has been apparent to me that the lives of Jefferson and Madison, and the mutual stimulation and support they provided each other, were so closely bound together that there was a certain artifice in dealing with one without the other. Yet it is easily understandable why scholars on the whole must do precisely that. Each of these great reflective statesmen created, in the course of a long life, an immense body of writings. A modern scholar's own lifetime may literally be too short to master the intricate content of these records and to assess the vast influence they exerted in their own day and subsequently in the history of this country from their day to our own.

The dual roles of Jefferson and Madison as thinkers and as men whose political careers proved to be decisive in forming the American Experiment along its fundamental moral lines help to suggest part of the difficulty that their interpreters face. These superb statesmen defined their ideas and doctrines in the press of urgent public problems of an unprecedented sort. Although they were philosophical and far-seeing, they wrote as men do who recognize the need to take reasoned positions in an unrelenting effort to mediate political conflicts or to meet grave crises. They could not be "free" of this concern and still create policy for the new American Republic. The miracle then is that they managed, in the midst of these limiting duresses, to transcend immediacy, to extend their insights to the more permanent and indeed the most extensive questions linking man to man, and America to mankind everywhere.

Consequently, one ascertains their "meaning" with marked trepidation. One does so, of course, on the basis of evidence, but evidence of a massive and multiform sort that makes disquieting demands on the interpreter to discriminate between the essential and nonessential, and to subdue the intricacy, plasticity, and apparent ambiguity of the overly detailed tapestry that is the record. Such difficulties are endemic to the historical enterprise, markedly so to that phase of it that goes by the somewhat overconfident label of "intellectual history." They are mentioned here because they exist in marked prominence for men who are philosopher–statesmen, and whose intellectual fecundity suffered no diminution in their late years of official "retirement" and unofficial zenith performance in reviewing and extending the principles of the American Experiment. They are also mentioned to highlight the inescapable fact that the chances for error, and the opportunities for finding in Jefferson and Madison what one is predisposed to find are abundant. I am not sure that I have peeled off the layers of the outer or conventional Madison to reveal the core of his concern and belief; I am only sure that I have tried to locate myself in what Emerson called the "angle of vision."

What has distressed me in the past has been the bland and shallow approach that ignores difficulties of this sort altogether, and assumes that James Madison is a construct from the text of his Tenth *Federalist* paper, or that he is—having been a retiring personality in the glare of the political publicity—a man one can safely relegate to purely official recognition as "father" of the Constitution. (Usually, those who make this explicit or silent judgment are the ones who also believe in their hearts that the Constitution is only "a piece of paper" and that decisions by the Judiciary have made our history independently of the "facade" of basic law.) In any event, both of these perspectives on Madison freeze him in one phase, and at one time, of his long and subtle journey of inquiry and understanding. To take but one relevant example: must we not attempt to account for the Madison who achieved leadership in the First Congress, observing what he thought to be profound errors in the Administration, and attempting to implement the principles and ideas of the American political system? The outcome of these political experiences was to sharpen his devotion to the liberal character of the American Experiment. He put those strongly democratic sentiments into new form in the essays he contributed to the *National Gazette* in 1790–91, defining the views of the opposition, the men who were already being called "the Republicans," although they were not yet, by modern criteria, a distinct, mature political party.

In 1795 Madison wrote an important political pamphlet which was published anonymously under the title *Political Observations*. In this review of the Administration's record in domestic financial policy and foreign economic policy, he probed the meaning of the American Experiment afresh. He stressed the rationale that lay behind the five-year campaign by what was then called the "Republican interest" (headed by Jefferson, as Secretary of State, and himself, as the recognized Congressional leader), to effect an export-import policy that would free American commerce from the fetters Great Britain had placed on it. His arguments for a discriminatory policy against Britain—as essentially a counterdiscrimination against it for crippling American trade—were fortified by Britain's recent, intolerable spoliations of the newly flourishing American commerce on the high seas in 1794. He moved on to questions of defense, arguing a modern defense posture but opposing war, and explicitly spoke out in support of continued friendship with revolutionary France, feeling, as did Jefferson, the obligation incurred by America to the country that had participated in its victorious war for Independence, and loath to turn its back on a "sister republic." What emerges from this political tract is a position that goes beyond the slogan "neutrality" to a larger view of an effectively independent nation.

Madison recommended that America exert pressure on Britain to make her dealings with her quondam colonies just. He envisaged such measures as the building of a strong merchant marine, support of domestic manufactures, and strategic commercial policies towards other nations, to achieve conditions favorable to American commerce.

Thus, even in this heated period of partisan politics Madison is found rethinking the meaning of an independent American Republic under constitutional government. In this period, and in the forty-odd years that comprise the second half of his life, he continued resolutely to reformulate his views. Not one single dictum, then, but many reasoned reflections await the inquiring scholar on basic questions like: the suffrage, the proper meaning of representation, majority rule and minority rights; property; equality; slavery and methods of emancipation; foreign policy; principles of liberty and of constitutional government, including the tricky question of rules for the interpretation of the Constitution. He also deepened his thought on the rules of political parties, on sectionalism, union, liberty, and learning. As a sophisticated critic of social thought, Madison's late years out of public office were equally brilliant as his earlier years in public service when he had formulated his great principles of civil and religious freedom and his design of federalism. Certainly the profile of Madison's mind, whatever the secret recesses that must defy the interpreter's skill, cannot be satisfactorily attempted by a bold and brash resolve to contemplate only, so to speak, the predominant train of ideas in a selected year or season.

Some such feeling, that Madison had been singularly deprived of study so far as his intellectual growth was concerned, was already present in my book, *Jefferson and Madison: The Great Collaboration* (1950). There I was concerned to establish the nature of the half-century friendship and collaboration of these two seminal minds in American political history. But in the intervening years I have acquired an increasingly lively interest in Madison, as a person and as a thinker, beyond what I possessed when I was trying to combat the fallacious image of him as a shadowy and distinctly second, younger protégé of Thomas Jefferson. What I tried to establish was the real partnership that existed between them and that made their joint influence a commanding political leadership in the forty years from Independence to the close of Madison's administration, and in their renewed partnership as private citizens, returned home at last to the humanistic interests of retired statesmen. That book closes, for instance, with an account of Jefferson's and Madison's labors to establish the University of Virginia, the "darling" project of Jefferson's last years.

The lectures on the occasion of the Whig–Clio Bicentennial gave me the opportunity I had been naturally turning toward, of coming to Madison afresh, in and for himself. I doubt that I will rest satisfied with what is essentially a cluster of three important themes of his political thought, for nothing short of a comprehensive intellectual portrait can preserve the valuable insights and wealth of moral–political criticism his lifelong learning provides. I offer these essays therefore as interim findings that at least carry me beyond what I perceived about Madison in the past, and that may possibly be of interest to others because they are more than episodes, more even than selected aspects of his thought; they are expressive of his caste of mind. These essays are, I feel, the beginning outline of his essential philosophy of politics and moral discourse. They function for him as George Santayana once described his own philosophy as characteristically his: "In the past or in the future, my language and my borrowed knowledge would have been different, but under whatever sky I had been born, since it is the same sky, I should have had the same philosophy."

Thus, each of the three themes I discuss was of intense interest to Madison, from the origin of his mature consciousness to the close of his speculations. In what does man's liberty consist, and how may it be advanced? How can liberty fulfill the demands of justice in an extensive and yet a regionally individualized society? What may we expect of free, self-governing men by way of loyalty to a union that promises their likeliest chance for happiness and well-being? Religious liberty Madison found to be the first component of human freedom, for if the mind and conscience are captive, the man is. Civil liberties presuppose religious liberty for Madison, and what a shorthand language calls the affairs of "church and state" stands for a wider context of respect for the inquiring, the *creative* creature. So marked a respect for the silences of man, for privacy and private judgment, was in no way conceived to mean a doctrine of absolute or irrational individualism. The "atom" individual against whom Tocqueville points an accusing finger does not frequent Madison's moral or political world. Proud to enroll himself in "the cause of liberty," Madison still brought an equal concern to his work for social justice, work which crystallized for him in the great test of devising the framework of fundamental law that would safeguard popular liberty for an extensive republic. Inquiry and experiment were the trying roads he, like all mortals, even the best among them, travelled. It suited such an active life of searching for means to all-important human ends that Madison should meet the most unyielding and relentless difficulties towards the close of his life. The heritage of liberty and justice is harder to preserve than establish! Especially so, since liberty is never "sufficient" and justice is constitutionally, incurably blind to one or another, to some claimants.

If the word is not needlessly frightening, I would say that the themes of this book—liberty, justice, and union—are *dialectically* related. Not in abstract, and not in a pattern we are familiar with as "thesis, antithesis, and synthesis": but in the sense I have indicated by the previous remarks.

Finally, I would call attention to the very great service Madison rendered in the last decade of life, a service that must be counted a glorious proof of the occasionally obscured truth that America needs its very old men if they are wise men, just as much as it needs its flaming and daring (and only to a minor degree its synthetic) youth. A frail and invalid former statesman, in his seventy-fifth year, was charged by his great friend, Thomas Jefferson: "Take care of me when dead." Madison, we must remember, was alone on the scene from 1826 to 1836—a decade of extraordinary crisis, full of the portent of the conflict that might disrupt the union and grind the great experiment to a halt. Madison spoke out—for himself, for Jefferson, for his country, as his last message, "Advice To My Country," dramatically underlines. His keen mind and profound judgment not only withdrew the name of his friend, and his own, from the ranks of the Southern nullifiers and secessionists, but made it possible for the nation to preserve itself *within* the vital symbolism of its spirit and laws.

Yet if we held Madison to a strict account, the vastly good final service he rendered his country was "inconsistent" with positions he had at times advocated in the past, and in the same way, although more markedly, "inconsistent" as interpretation of the views of Thomas Jefferson. What one makes of this pecksniff discovery depends upon the degree of historical imagination brought to the act of criticism—that of sledgehammer literalness? or something like the tempered subtlety adequate to human experience? The latter ideal would demand a bow to this last service of Madison's, on the ground that his reformulated views, if not in the interest of exact fact and literal truth, were the penetrating judgments a man makes of that ideal he hoped to serve throughout the course of his life, and what he gauged in the interest of the lifelong friend who wrote "Take care of me when dead," to be Jeffersonian principles—not by Jefferson's words of the immediate occasion or context, but "on the whole" and "in the spirit of."

This kind of essential truth about a man is neither a higher truth in the mystical sense nor a whitewash, although one should stand prepared for the brittle outcry of minds that cannot see any truth save a literalistic one. To such minds, of course, Madison and Madison's final review of what Jefferson *really* meant present a tissue of evil deceit or hypocrisy insteady of an honorable message, full of the human predicament of men who will not bring themselves to permit the destruction of *imperfectly* free society in order to "save" an illusory freedom—whether for the states, for the individual, or, in ultimate irony, for nobody and no good. If Madison reversed his earlier "doctrine" (in the narrow sense) of "state rights" and "strict construction," he stood true to the bright vision of human happiness that had lighted the awesome burdens placed on him throughout his life by his discipleship in the art of free society.

ADRIENNE KOCH

Washington, D.C.
June 11, 1965

ACKNOWLEDGMENTS

THIS STUDY was made possible by a fellowship from the Rockefeller Foundation, in their program of legal and political philosophy. I am grateful to the Foundation for its support.

The Bicentennial Committee of the Whig–Clio Society of Princeton, in inviting me to give the Bicentennial Lectures on James Madison, provided a welcome challenge to present some of the material I had been preparing. I am grateful to Professor Wilbur S. Howell, Chairman of the Board of Trustees of the American Whig–Clio Society, and to Morgan Kousser, Chairman of the Undergraduate Committee for the Whig–Clio Bicentennial, for inviting me to Princeton on this interesting occasion.

During my stay in Princeton, everything possible was done to make it a joyous as well as a memorable visit. I should like to thank particularly Professor and Mrs. Julian P. Boyd and Professor Alpheus T. Mason for their generous attentions and gracious hospitality.

CONTENTS

Chapter One: Liberty

"The art of free society consists first in the maintenance of the symbolic code; and secondly in fearlessness of revision, to secure that the code serves those purposes which satisfy an enlightened reason. Those societies which cannot combine reverence to their symbols with freedom of revision, must ultimately decay either from anarchy, or from the slow atrophy of a life stifled by useless shadows."

Alfred North Whitehead
Symbolism (1927)

Liberty

As a young man of eighteen, James Madison rode north from Orange to Princeton, one of the first Southern students to enter the College of New Jersey. His earliest letter extant is dated Nassau-Hall, August 10, 1769, apparently written shortly after his arrival, to his former tutor and family friend, the Reverend Thomas Martin, himself a New Jersey College graduate and the one who probably had much to do with Madison's decision to attend. Madison reported:

> I am perfectly pleased with my present situation; and the prospect before me of three years confinement, however terrible it may sound, has nothing in it, but what will be greatly alleviated by the advantages I hope to derive from it.[1]

The three-year confinement brought the advantages he had dutifully anticipated, but far beyond what his tone implied. Staying on after his graduation for an extra semester, Madison became the first of a long line of the species of rare American bird known as "graduate students." The habits of the scholar, the foibles of academic men, and the wide world of theology, philosophy, morality, politics, history, languages, had made their mark on him.

Madison carried this invisible freight back with him to Montpelier. But he would cross and recross his steps, north and south, to Williamsburg, Philadelphia, Annapolis, New York, his familiar Princeton again, and in time—to Washington, and then home to the Blue Ridge beauty of his plantation. Each step of the way meant "confinement . . . greatly alleviated by advantages." More often than not, the advantages were for others. And Madison was a learner all his life. Patrick Henry, his enemy, saw the young Princetonian and flung at him the contemptuous phrase "a theoretic statesman." But it was Henry who fell behind, unable to meet the inexorable demands of patience, knowledge, and wisdom that "the great transactions" of the age required.

And James Madison, as he deepened in experience, developed an increasing grasp of theory, fact, and the refinements of a subtle man. The instinct to serve his country, tested by forty years of indispensable service, in domestic and foreign affairs, could not die. When he was eighty-three years old, therefore, he surveyed the dangerous divisions that beset the American Republic with which his life had been bound up, and wrote an earnest last message for posthumous publication. He called it "Advice To My Country." It reads:

> As this advice, if it ever see the light will not do it till I am no more, it may be considered as issuing from the tomb, where truth alone can be respected, and the happiness of man alone consulted. It will be entitled therefore to whatever weight can be derived from good intentions, and from the experience of one who has served his country in various stations through a period of forty years, who espoused in his youth and adhered through his life to the cause of its liberty, and who has borne a part in most of the great transactions which will constitute epochs of its destiny.
>
> The advice nearest to my heart and deepest in my convictions is that the Union of the States be cherished and perpetuated. Let the open enemy to it be regarded as a Pandora with her box opened; and the disguised one, as the Serpent creeping with his deadly wiles into Paradise.[2]

This solemn warning is truly Madison's advice to America. It is a terse but ultimate summation for posterity, of the prime purposes and values which directed his life. The message provides a matrix from which I have selected three aspects of Madison's thought and career. The first chapter considers Madison in his younger years, when "the cause of liberty" won his devotion. The second reflects on one of "the great transactions" of history, possibly the greatest, in which Madison became a principal actor, the work of his middle years, when he devoted himself to designing a new model for a just society. The concluding chapter deals with the specific bearings of his last message of advice to his country, the momentous years when Madison, though an old man, made his paramount concern the preservation of the union.

2

Liberty is my first subject—one of those questions according to David Hume, "which have been canvassed and disputed with great eagerness since the first origin of science and philosophy," so that we should have been able "in the course of two thousand years . . . to pass from words to the true and real subject of the controversy." In disgust with this "labyrinth of obscure sophistry," Hume pronounced the question of liberty and necessity as in effect "metaphysical," and turned from such fruitless contest to issues of common life and experience.

Nothing so formidable as the *metaphysical* question of liberty and necessity need concern us here. Our context will be the world where real fire burns and real persecution makes sacred the cry for liberty.

Madison, in his "Advice To My Country," permitted himself to mention his lifelong adherence to "the cause of liberty." Invariably he included in that phrase a reference to its double aspect, of civil and religious liberty. I will concentrate on Madison's efforts to establish religious liberty because his thought and feeling on this question were matters of great moment to him. An analysis of them is peculiarly important, at least for two reasons. First, it is basic to an understanding of Madison's character and of his entire *weltanschauung,* if I may use that apt but unlovely word. Second, since Madison's work has been resorted to so prominently in our generation by the Supreme Court in cases involving religious liberty, it is of great practical consequence that his position be understood.

No one can know exactly how Madison came

to feel and think as he did about religious freedom. But the best guess leads us, I suspect, to within a few feet of Whig Hall on the Princeton campus. William Cabell Rives, Madison's friend and first biographer, was the first to suggest that Madison deliberately chose Princeton rather than nearby William and Mary College, because the latter was distasteful to him for the High Church Toryism of its President.[3] On the other hand, the year before Madison's choice took shape, the College of New Jersey had come under the administration of the illustrious Reverend Dr. John Witherspoon, the learned, productive, and apparently omnicompetent Scotch educator. Moreover, the College had already established a reputation as the religious and educational capital of Presbyterian America. Finally, Madison's inclination towards Princeton may well have been fortified by its political reputation, for the campus had come to be known as a center of enthusiastic patriotism which knew no charity for Crown or Mitre.

What matters more than *why* Madison came to Princeton is what happened to him there. Plaudits again for Dr. Witherspoon! This good educator, having arrived in America and settled in the colonial college at Princeton, with its 120 students and its one spacious Nassau Hall, quickly formed an ardent attachment for his new world. He proceeded to build up the college, and to introduce liberal and modern educational innovations, such as the teaching of French and mathematics. Dr. Witherspoon himself insisted upon instruction in the *English* language. He deliberately cultivated a clear, direct, and understandable style in his own lectures and seminars; this represented not only an innovation at that time but a delightful concession to the sorely tried students of that day. He also exerted his influence on the philosophical scene to steer a middle course between idealism and materialism in the enlightened Scottish tradition known as "Common Sense Realism."

Witherspoon had studied with David Hume, Adam Smith, and Thomas Reid. The Scottish Enlightenment in moral philosophy and social scientific areas, therefore, became a philosophic must for the students at old Nassau Hall.

Meanwhile, the personal influence of the "good old Doctor" meant more than one can calculate. Madison's ambition to do his utmost in his studies may be taken as a tribute to his excellent preceptor. In an autobiographical statement in his late years Madison described his rigorous regimen of study, taking double the course load, as an "indiscreet experiment of the minimum of sleep and the maximum of application which the constitution would bear." In explication, he said that he was reduced for some weeks "to less than five hours [of sleep] in the twenty-four." [4]

It seems clear that the restrained Presbyterianism of Dr. Witherspoon's administration, and his favorite maxim that "college administrators should govern—but not too much," did not suffocate the generation of coming statesmen, educators, lawyers, and ministers who were his devoted students. But Madison's college career included other activities besides diligent study. One time-consuming occupation that did not show up in Madison's circumspect time sheet was the "paper war" between the Whigs and the Clios, into which Madison entered with glee, contributing at least three, long, mock-classical verses, full of a contrived and sophomorically coarse humor. We must also remember the friendly attachments that grew out of student debates and discussions, including some fairly soul-searching philosophical ones. We know these took place for example on the metaphysical question of liberty and necessity (Hume's warning of its fruitlessness notwithstanding) by the surviving correspondence between Madison and his friendly young tutor, Samuel Stanhope

Smith, who later became President of Princeton. On the whole, Madison's close ties with college friends—Smith, William Bradford, Philip Freneau, Hugh Henry Breckenridge, and so many others—sustained him in the traumatic after-years that follow upon the close of a college career, and reached far into his life, giving him the support of membership in an affectionate community where significant ideas and ideals had been explored and shared. As token of this cherished ring of friendship, Madison may be seen some sixty years after he left Princeton, in corresponding with another Witherspoon student, planning a new system of higher education for Kentucky. Indeed, in innumerable political and cultural projects and causes, Madison found himself shoulder to shoulder with "old Princetonians," and he came to count on them as a kind of advance guard, not only in Virginia affairs, but throughout the South, ready to join him in legislative battles, political contests, and in his perpetual programs instructing public opinion.

Madison's "indiscreet experiment" apparently did not slake his appetite for studies. After graduation he remained at Princeton for another half year or so of study under Dr. Witherspoon's direction, adding a little Hebrew to his knowledge of classical languages and literature, reading in theology, and continuing his inquiries into moral philosophy and political history and thought. As one of the students who had attended his own graduation garbed defiantly in cloth of American manufacture, to show the earnestness of the nonimportation campaign, Madison was not an "ivory tower" student. Moreover, although we know he gained much knowledge and teaching by example from Witherspoon and two or three of the excellent tutors who second-stopped him, there *was* a stubborn streak of independent critical scrutiny in the slight young Virginian that made him unreceptive to mere fellowship. Thus he surreptitiously read the forbidden Voltaire while he was at Princeton. He also prepared a set of notes on logic and epistemology which he titled "A Brief System of Logic" that show not only an admirable grasp of these subjects, but that he could not accept uncritically even "the great Mr. Locke"—nor *anyone*, for that matter.[5]

In summing up what Princeton meant to Madison's intellectual development, I would suggest that it made of him a devoted American student of Enlightenment thought. But the point is that he had emancipated himself to welcome the *spirit* of the Enlightenment, not swallow its dogmas; and that spirit is best expressed in the Kantian maxim: "*Dare to know*" (Audeo sapere). Not authority, but *reason* as instructed by *experience* was what Madison intended to rely on for truth in matters of nature and emphatically also in human nature and society. Once he was home in Virginia, Madison considered various careers, including the profession of law. But more and more he returned to "the principles and modes of government," for it was not private law practice he desired but public law, that supreme and dangerous sport of plunging a hook into Leviathan.

3

The first test of Madison's commitment to religious liberty "found a particular occasion for its exercise in the persecution instituted in his County as elsewhere against the preachers belonging to the sect of Baptists then beginning to spread thro the country." The Madison Autobiography continues:

> "Notwithstanding the enthusiasm which contributed to render them obnoxious to sober opinion as well as to the laws then in force, against Preachers dissenting from the Established Religion, he spared no exertion to save

them from imprisonment and to promote their release from it. This interposition tho' a mere duty prescribed by his conscience, obtained for him a lasting place in the favor of that particular sect." [6]

The story persists that Madison never forgot his childhood experience of hearing a Baptist preacher deliver a sermon to passersby through the iron grates of his jail window! The sensitive boy needed no books to see the gross repugnance of laws that put honest men in jail for their ultimate personal beliefs about the Creator.

In any case, by April of 1774 Madison had thought so long and hard about the meaning of religious liberty that he wrote to his Princeton friend, Billy Bradford in Philadelphia, envying him for living where the privileges of religious liberty might be enjoyed, while he as a Virginian had to contend with a country stifled and deprived of those "generous principles." He then penned an eloquent passage elaborating the good consequences already visible in Philadelphia from its "generous principles" of religious liberty:

> Foreigners have been encouraged to settle among you. Industry and Virtue have been promoted by mutual emulations and mutual

Inspection, Commerce and the Arts have flourished and I can not help attributing those continual exertions of Genius which appear among you to the inspiration of Liberty and that love of Fame and Knowledge which always accompany it. Religious bondage shackles and debilitates the mind and unfits it for every noble enterprise every expanded prospect.[7]

Madison's part "in the great transactions" of history began when he was elected a delegate from Orange County to the Revolutionary Convention in Williamsburg in the late spring of 1776. He was a junior member, twenty-five years old, circumspect and shy, but he was already known to a few of his colleagues for his enlightened beliefs and formidable reputation for learning. Thus in spite of his youth, he was assigned to the committee to frame "a declaration of rights, and such a plan of government as will be most likely to maintain peace and order in this colony, and secure substantial and equal liberty to the people." The famous Virginia Declaration of Rights served as a model for subsequent American constitutions and was reprinted and circulated throughout America, in England, and on the Continent. George Mason was the principal draftsman, but Madison, as we shall see, left a memorable impress.

In one article of the Declaration of Rights, Mason had drafted a provision that ". . . all men should enjoy the fullest Toleration in the Exercise of Religion according to the dictates of conscience." Madison felt that this provision for toleration fell disappointingly short of "*the generous principles*" in which he believed. He therefore wrote a substitute provision which read, in part, that ". . . all men are equally entitled to the full and free exercise of it [religion] according to the dictates of conscience; and *therefore* that no man or class of men ought, on account of religion to be invested with peculiar emoluments or privileges. . . ." Madison was hesitant to address the Convention and sought an important sponsor to strengthen the chances of adoption. He chose Patrick Henry to move it, but Henry rapidly gave ground in the debate when he was angrily asked whether he intended to disestablish the church, and the amendment lost. Madison then drafted another amendment, which declared merely that "all men are equally entitled to enjoy the free exercise of religion." This amendment passed and became part of the Virginia Declaration of Rights.[8]

To realize the significance of Madison's contribution, one should take note of at least the following essential points: First, the linguistic change from toleration to religious freedom marks the beginning of a major break with previous liberal political thought. John Locke's influential doctrine of religious liberty had simply called for toleration.[9] Perhaps the best brief formulation of the defective nature of toleration as such was stated by Thomas Paine: "Toleration," he wrote, "is not the *opposite* of Intolerance, but it is the *counterfeit* of it. Both are despotisms. The one assumes to itself the right of withholding Liberty of Conscience, and the other of granting it."[10] This advance on the European liberal tradition in itself should invalidate the conventional wisdom which asserts that American political thought is purely derivative, and nothing more than "Locke writ large." It is to Madison's credit that he came to this position on the basis of his own reflection.

Second, Madison was not the only American to reach this position. Jefferson had already come to the divide between toleration and freedom, as is clearly shown in his draft of a Virginia Constitution which he sent to the Convention from his seat in Congress, in Philadelphia. Jefferson chafed at being detained in the

Continental Congress because he believed that "the whole object of the present controversy" was the work of framing a new government. Nevertheless, the draft he submitted was considered at a late point on the floor of the Convention, and as the editor of the Jefferson Papers, Julian Boyd, discovered, "more of Jefferson's constitution was incorporated in the Virginia Constitution than he remembered or most historians have discerned." [11] It is Mr. Boyd's judgment, also, that the adoption of Jefferson's provisions on religious freedom, if they had been adopted, would have spared years of grinding legislative struggle to secure full religious freedom. To a great extent, this may also be said of Madison's original amendment.

Third, Madison's efforts in the Virginia Convention could not have gone unnoticed by Thomas Jefferson. Their shared beliefs on so profound a principle as religious freedom became a powerful bond which initially ranged them alongside each other and led to the close friendship and remarkable half-century collaboration between them. In this, as in many later instances, we see each man reaching positions independently as the result of private inquiry and meditation. We also see what became a pattern of mutual re-enforcement and fraternity that made their joint efforts a formidable force in winning each step towards an open society.

Fourth, we see in Madison's strategy at the very opening of his public career a trait that was indispensable to all his achievements. We may call it an attitude of strategic or creative compromise. Madison's style of conduct involved a commitment to basic principles and a recognition of the diverse and conflicting interests which have a claim to be recognized in any just solution. He operated with the rule that at times half a loaf was all that could be purchased; and yet such a transaction was for him a purchase on the installment plan. Thus, having gained a *declaration* of religious liberty over toleration, but having failed in securing and implementing full religious freedom, he prepared himself for the next encounters.

4

The next stage in Madison's continuing struggle for religious liberty culminated in two classic pronouncements: Jefferson's *Bill for Establishing Religious Freedom,* which had been submitted to the Virginia Legislature in 1779, but was not enacted; and Madison's *Memorial and Remonstrance Against Religious Assessments.* A new crisis was reached in 1784 when Patrick Henry introduced an *Assessment Bill*. The Bill proposed to support the Christian Church without naming any particular denomination, by giving each taxpayer the privilege of designating which church should receive his share of the tax. There is irony in the fact that the mighty Patrick Henry, to whom Madison had turned as sponsor for his original amendment on religious liberty, was now facing him as the leader of the new forces for state support of religion.

Although it was a polite eighteenth century world, it is not difficult to detect the unmistakable configuration of the political gravy train in the measure. Madison picked up just this aspect when he wrote that the Presbyterians, previously the enemies of Establishment, would now join forces with the Anglicans, as eager "to set up an establishment which is to take them in, as they were to pull down that which shut them out." What gave the battle epic proportions was the lineup of luminaries behind Henry, including Washington, John Marshall, and Richard Henry Lee.[12] The bill all but passed, except that Madison and his supporters managed to get deferment of its final consideration until November 1785.

In this interval, Madison composed his *Memo-*

rial and Remonstrance at the suggestion of George Nicholas, who wrote him that although a majority of the counties were for the bill, a majority of the people were against it. An able protest and petition would give the people a chance to speak.[13] Nicholas was exultant when he read Madison's astute and yet stirring appeal, circulated it at once throughout the state, where it was read and signed by thousands of the formerly voiceless people.[14]

What were the potent ingredients Madison put into the *Remonstrance* to effect such extensive change? In general, the position he developed we may call the plenary interpretation of freedom of thought which Jefferson had expressed in his Bill. Freedom of religion is essential because of the nature of man and the nature of human thought. Men are reasonable creatures who inquire before they believe. To *compel* them to believe, without respect for what appears to them to be sufficient or convincing evidence, will perhaps exact outward obedience but it will not produce belief. The Assessment Bill, said Madison, "violates the equality which ought to be the basis of every law." If we wish freedom for ourselves to choose, profess and observe the religion which we believe to be of divine origin, "we cannot deny an equal freedom to those whose minds have not yet yielded to the evidence which has convinced us." This represents one level, which I believe to be the fundamental one, of Madison's position. It provides the basis for exhibiting the error of assigning to political rulers the judgment of what is and what is not "religious truth." Madison is echoing the ancient question of free men, the typical "Who shall judge?" In his own language, "the bill implies either that the Civil Magistrate is a competent Judge of Religious truth; or that he may employ Religion as an engine of Civil policy. The first is an arrogant pretension falsified by the contradictory opinions of Rulers of all ages, and throughout the world: The second an unhallowed perversion of the means of salvation." [15]

Madison knew that his readers were almost entirely Christian believers of various sorts and he deliberately addressed much of the overt argument in the *Remonstrance* to the common fears of insecurity of a diversified Christian community. On this level, he spoke of what man owed to God, and what was an offence against God: "It is the duty of every man to render to the Creator such homage, and such only, as he believes to be acceptable to him," he wrote. "It . . . is a contradiction to the Christian religion itself, for every page of it *disavows* a dependence on the powers of the world" (italics added). Tax support of religion is also factually poor policy, "for it is known that this Religion both existed and flourished, not only without the support of human laws, but in spite of every opposition from them." What was wrong? Were men losing confidence in the innate excellence of their religion, were they "too conscious of its fallacies, to trust it to its own merits"? he asked. As for history, have we not seen that ecclesiastical establishments have made a wreck of human freedom? In some instances "they have been seen to erect a spiritual tyranny on the ruins of Civil authority; in many instances they have been seen upholding the thrones of political tyranny; in no instance have they been seen the guardians of the liberties of the people."

Revolutionary pride and memories were also skillfully enlisted by Madison's appeal. He urged his readers to "take alarm *at the first experiment* on our liberties," reminding them that "the freemen of America did not wait till usurped power had . . . entangled the question in precedents" (italics added). They foresaw "all the consequences in the principle, and they avoided the consequences by denying the principle" he asserted. Then he asked a question, using hauntingly familiar terms. "*Who* does not see that the same authority which can establish Christianity, in exclusion of all other Religions, may establish with the same ease any particular sect of Christians, in exclusion of all other Sects? That the same authority which can force a citizen to contribute three pence only of his property for the support of any one establishment, may force him to conform to any other establishment in all cases whatsoever?" (italics added). The taunt, in these terms, recalling the three pence tax on tea, and the offensive language of the Declaratory Act of 1766, which had asserted the right of Parliament to make laws binding the colonists "in all cases whatsoever," was unmistakable. Madison was provoking the memories of past tryanny to suggest the true character of what otherwise might be mistaken as a relatively innocuous and inexpensive law for support of Christian churches. Usurped power and tyranny were precisely what he charged against the big step backward that Henry's bill proposed.

Madison invited his readers to assume for a moment that such a bill were to become law—what then? Its practical effect on society, on morality, on the meaning of the American Experiment in independence and freedom would be corrosive and incurable. Good-bye to that generous policy of "offering an asylum to the persecuted and oppressed of every nation and religion—a policy which promised a lustre to the free United States, unknown in the old states of Europe. Instead of this policy, such a law would degrade from the equal rank of Citizens all those whose opinions in Religion do not bend to those of the Legislative authority." Unhappily, torrents of blood had been spilled in the old world "by vain attempts to extinguish Religious discord by proscribing all differences in Religious opinions." No American would want to tread that tragic and impossible road. Insistently, throughout this remarkable composition, Madison managed to put men on their mettle, cueing them to remember their best traditions and high moments of courage. But he did not fail to play upon their fears of encirclement, and thus he captured both natures of man. He had opened his address with the language of natural rights and placed the freedom of conscience at the head of all others. He closed with a recall of the same theme, calling attention to the principles of the *Declaration of Rights*, and asking whether the present legislature had the authority to "sweep away all our fundamental rights." If not, the right of every citizen to the free exercise of his religion must remain inviolate. "Either we must say that they [the Legislature] may control the freedom of the press, may abolish the trial by jury, may swallow up the Executive and Judiciary Powers of the State; nay that they may despoil us of our very right of suffrage, and erect themselves into an independent and hereditary assembly; or we must say that they have no authority to enact into law the Bill under consideration." All in all, it was quite a performance for a retiring scholar who had been trained in the debates between the Whigs and Clios and come from Princeton to the service of his State.

Madison's *Remonstrance* received overwhelming support and the pile of signed petitions delivered to the Assembly killed the Assessment Bill. Madison then moved in with Jefferson's *Bill for Religious Freedom* and had it enacted with a substantial majority. Then in January 1786, he hastened to send the triumphant news to Jefferson in Paris: "The enacting clauses passed without a single alteration, and I flatter myself have in this country extinguished forever the ambitious hope of making laws for the human mind." In the light of this reference to the enacting clauses, it is helpful to give the exact language of the basic one: "that all men shall be free to profess, and by argument to maintain, their opinions in matters of religion, and that the same shall in no wise diminish, enlarge, or affect their civil capacities." [16] The full meaning of this key clause is elaborated in Jefferson's *Notes on Virginia*, where he wrote: "The legitimate powers of government extend to such acts only as are injurious to others. But it does me no injury for my neighbor to say there are twenty gods, or no god. It neither picks my pocket nor breaks my leg." [17]

After Jefferson's death, Madison summed up the transcendent importance of the Act and its significance for a free society. "This act . . . was always held by Mr. Jefferson to be one of his best efforts in the Cause of Liberty to which he was devoted. And it is certainly the strongest legal barrier that could be erected against the connection of Church and State so fatal to the liberty of both."

5

The culmination of Madison's efforts in the cause of religious liberty was reached with his sponsorship of the Bill of Rights, including the all-important First Amendment in the first Congress under the Constitution. Given Madison's position, questions have been raised as to why he failed to make this move earlier—for example, in the Federal Convention itself. It is essential to answer these questions because Madison is sometimes represented as a man more concerned for the rights of property than for human rights. This charge cannot survive a careful study of Madison's sentiments, reasons, and conduct. One should at least take account of the actualities of the Constitutional Convention and Madison's mission therein before pronouncing judgment.

First, there were more than enough grave differences within the Convention to bring it to the breaking point on several occasions. To pursue the question of religious liberty at *that* time would have required a virtually impossible effort in trying to reconcile the differences among the states. Some states had religious establishments; others had toleration; and Virginia had a famous law guaranteeing complete religious freedom. Second, Madison believed that the general government possessed only delegated powers and therefore lacked the shadow of a claim to interfere with those states which had bills of rights. Third, and most important, Madison had come to see the ineffectiveness of a bill of rights even in his own state of Virginia, if that declaration of principles existed without implementing legislation to enforce its provisions. Finally, when late in the Convention George Mason did move for a bill of rights, the states unanimously voted against it.[18]

But we know that Madison's failure to act on this issue in the Convention, for whatever strategic reasons, was only a delaying action and certainly not an abandonment of his major principles. Two factors, however, made him review and change his strategy. In the course of his correspondence with Jefferson, he had come to see the feasibility of *enforcing* a written bill of rights by resorting to judicial review, Jefferson having suggested "the legal check which it [the constitution] puts into the hands of judiciary." [19] In addition, Madison became impressed by the extent and vociferousness of the demands for a bill of rights throughout the country, both in the press and in the state ratifying conventions. It is significant that he obtained the critical vote for ratification by Virginia after he pledged that he would work for a bill of rights when the new government was established.[20] In his campaign for a seat in the new Congress, Madison made a similar campaign promise.

Madison kept his word. Recognizing the delicacy and dangers that lurked in this difficult task, Madison urged, despite the opposition he encountered, that the bill of rights question be one of the first orders of business in the First Federal Congress. He was fully aware that there had been at least two major forces feeding into the demands for a bill of rights during the ratification process. One might be termed the *manifest* content of the demand—the effort to protect basic and precious civil liberties from possible future encroachment by the federal government. The second might be termed the *latent* content of the demand—the effort to shear the powers of the federal government, even in some cases to cripple or annihilate it. Madison's intricate task therefore was to ride herd on those in Congress who would make use of the issue of the bill of rights to weaken the Constitution, but to urge forward those who would support the genuine subject matter of civil liberties. The tightrope Madison walked in the many committee discussions and revisions of the proposed amendments signified his effort to reconcile liberty with authority, to safeguard the unalienable rights of man without weakening or rendering useless the requisite energy of the federal government.

Freedom of thought in its three aspects of

religious freedom, freedom of speech and a free press were Madison's first and paramount concern in his fight for the Bill of Rights. His initial draft, as it respected religious freedom, was introduced in this form:

> The civil rights of none shall be abridged on account of religious belief or worship, nor shall any national religion be established, nor shall the full and equal rights of conscience be in any manner, or on any pretext, abridged.[21]

A complicated legislative process then ensued, resulting in the religious clause of the First Amendment. It is necessary to add, however, that Madison had proposed an *additional* amendment on religion—one that was original with him and not proposed by any of the states. This proposed amendment he considered "the most valuable on the whole list."[22] It declared that "no state shall violate the equal rights of conscience, or the freedom of the press or the trial by jury in criminal cases." Madison explicitly argued that if it was necessary to restrain the national government, it was equally essential to place checks on the state governments, since some states did not have a bill of rights. Passed by the House, the proposal was later eliminated by the

Senate. There is no doubt, therefore, that Madison maintained his sovereign faith in religious liberty and that the combined effect of his two proposed amendments would have invalidated any material encroachment by the federal and even state governments in the domain of religious liberty. It is hardly necessary to remark that Madison's two amendments combined would have advanced the cause of effective human rights at a greatly accelererated pace over what its actual history became. It would doubtless have had other interesting effects, among them an explicit commitment by the father of the Constitution to a basic limitation upon the rights of the states.

6

Madison was so zealous to regulate his practice by his profound commitment to the ideal of religious freedom that a far longer chapter than this would be needed to enumerate and analyze his practice. Let me cite only a few telling instances, from three periods of his later life.

In his "Autobiography" Madison called attention to his position in the First Federal Congress when he stated his disapproval of having

"Chaplains to Congress paid out of the public Treasury as a violation of principle. He thought the only legitimate and becoming mode would be that of a voluntary contribution from the members." [23]

During his Presidency, Madison agreed with Jefferson that it was against the spirit of religious freedom to proclaim any public day of thanksgiving or prayer. In the opening of the War of 1812, Congress and the orthodox among the public began to murmur at the President's failure to proclaim a day of public humiliation and prayer for victory. Congress then passed a resolution recommending that the President appoint such a day, and only then did the reluctant President act. He must have given his action a bit of thought, because instead of calling on the people to pray, he proclaimed that he was designating a day in response to a request by Congress, to permit the religious societies "so disposed, to offer, at one and the same time, their common vows and adorations to Almighty God, on the solemn occasion produced by the war, in which he has been pleased to permit the injustice of a foreign Power to involve these United States." [24] The witticism at the end was directed against his Federalist enemies, particularly the Governor of Massachusetts, who had called for prayers *against* the war which it had "pleased the Almighty Ruler of the world . . . to permit us to be engaged in . . . against the nation from which we are descended."

The situation began to be an annual affair. In 1813 Congress again requested the President for a public day of prayer. He repeated his cautious and corrective language, this time calling for "All who shall be piously disposed" to give thanks. He added "If the public homage of a people can ever be worthy the favorable regard of the Holy and Omniscient Being to whom it is addressed, it must be that in which those who join in it are guided only by their free choice, by the impulse of their hearts and the dictates of their consciences." Freewill offerings alone "can be acceptable to Him whom no hypocrisy can deceive and no forced sacrifices propitiate." [25]

Far more important, however, were the two veto messages which President Madison sent to Congress in February 1811. The first rejected a bill entitled "An act incorporating the Protestant Episcopal Church in the town of Alexandria in the District of Columbia." He gave two interesting grounds for this veto. First, "Because the bill exceeds the rightful authority to which governments are limited by the essential distinction between civil and religious functions, and violates in particular the article of the Constitution of the United States which declares that 'Congress shall make no law respecting a religious establishment.'" Second, "Because the bill vests in the said incorporated church an authority to provide for the support of the poor and the education of poor children of the same, an authority which, being altogether superfluous if the provision is to be the result of pious charity, would be a precedent for giving to religious societies as such a legal agency on carrying into effect a public and civil duty."[26]

In his retirement after the Presidency, Madison worked with Jefferson in planning the University of Virginia. They were in perfect accord on the decision to make it a strictly secular university devoted to "the illimitible freedom of the human mind," in Jefferson's phrase, "a temple" in Madison's words, "dedicated to science and liberty," "a nursery of scholars and patriots." In 1823 Madison had occasion to write to Edward Everett of Harvard on the subject of religion in education: he commented on the "difficulty of reconciling the Christian mind to the absence of a religious tuition from a university established by law, and at the common expense," adding that the difficulty was probably "less with us than with you. The settled opinion here is that religion is essentially distinct from civil government, and exempt from its cognizance; the connection between them is injurious to both." [27]

7

I now turn to Madison's final and considered formulation of his beliefs on the relationship between religion and civil government. This formulation appeared in a long letter written in the evening of his life, in 1833, to the Reverend Jasper Adams, then President of the College of Charleston. It merits close attention because of the importance of the subject, both for Madison and our own current concerns and because the letter has never been dealt with before.[28]

Dr. Adams sent Madison a copy of his pamphlet, "The Relations of Christianity to Civil Government in the United States," and requested the aged statesman's comments. Adams argued against the doctrine "that Christianity has no connection with our civil constitutions of government" and maintained that "the people of the United States have retained the Christian religion as the foundation of their civil, legal, and political institutions." On the basis of what he called an inductive examination of colonial history, the state constitutions and of the First Amendment, Adams concluded that we do indeed have a national religion, although one that is tolerant of all Christian denominations. But he lamented that the view was gaining ground that religion and government had no connection with each other and found this view "in the highest degree pernicious in its tendency" to all our institutions, pervasively corrupting the morals of the American people.

Madison conscientiously studied Adams' argument, because he evidently still found the subject intensely important. He found that it contained a frontal attack on the position which he and Jefferson had worked out as the essential contribution of the American political Enlightenment, an attack generally on a lofty plane, naming no names (except an occasional footnote where Adams permitted himself to single out Jefferson for censure) but repudiating the great principle of a new secular order. Madison consequently considered his own comment carefully, as is indicated not only by the thoughtful letter he wrote, but by the fact that he bothered to handwrite it himself, despite the fact that his chronic rheumatism "makes my hands and fingers as averse to the pen as they are awkward in the use of it." The letter was marked "private." It cannot, therefore, be interpreted as a stance taken for public notice.

Madison judged that the central question was: does the Christian religion, assuming that it is the best and purest religion, require financial aid from the government? In answering the question, he said he would "waive" all arguments based on natural rights and social compact theory. He would confine himself to an inductive examination of the sort advocated by Reverend Adams (more in theory, Madison felt, than in practice). He himself gladly resorted to inductive grounds because "on this question experience will be an admitted Umpire, the more adequate as the connections between government and religion have existed in various degrees and forms, and now can be compared with examples where connection has been entirely dissolved." Accordingly, he began by citing the Papal system as the worst government, because "government and religion are . . . consolidated." He next reviewed those European governments where government and religion were not completely consolidated, but where there was an established church and very little toleration of other churches. He observed that that system favored neither religion nor government. A third type of relationship was exemplified by Holland, where "the experiment of combining a liberal toleration with the establishment of a particular creed" had recently been tried.

Despite these gradations among European states, in Madison's considered judgment, it remained for North America "to bring the great and interesting subject to a fair, and finally a decisive test." He pointed out that the American Colonies had in at least five important instances—Rhode Island, Pennsylvania, New Jersey, Delaware, and the greater part of New York—existed without a religious establishment, relying upon voluntary contributions entirely to support religion. He suggested that the religious condition of these colonies certainly bore favorable comparison with the other colonies where religious establishments of one sort or another existed. But these colonial ventures, however encouraging, could not be taken as decisive. Some would argue that their experiments were conducted under the control of a foreign government whose own "reasons of state" may have dictated the experiments and that the "tendency" of religious liberty could not be reliably inferred from them. Madison also noted that they lacked "the full scope necessary"—both in terms of *full* religious freedom, and in terms of steady and settled policy—to constitute a test of the consequences of the separation of church and state. No, on all counts the best test was the testimony derivable from the post-Revolutionary period when one could fairly examine the effects of deliberate and complete separation of church and state in certain parts of the independent United States.

Madison began by calling attention to the New England states, a region certainly not notable in its colonial past for religious liberty, and still (in 1833) not up to that demanding standard. Even in this case, however, Madison thought there had been improvement—successive relaxations of the old pattern of religious establishment and intermingling of religious and governmental concerns and authority. He found these relaxations devoid of "evidence of disadvantage either to religion or to good government."

Without question it was "the Southern states" that furnished the best test of the effects of disestablishment and full religious freedom. Prior to the Declaration of Independence, they had been fettered by a legal provision for the support of religion; after Independence, they had turned to "a spontaneous support" of religion by the people—or no support, if they so chose. As he himself, armed with the memory of "before" and "after," could testify, the effect had been altogether salutary. The pastors had become more notable for greater purity and industry; their "flocks" more devoted than they had been when compelled to support religious worship. The contrast was especially striking in Virginia, which had blazed the way in the experiment for complete religious freedom. Virginia's experience demonstrated beyond reasonable doubt that religion clearly did not require the support of government, and that government in no way suffered "by the exemption of religion from its cognizance or its pecuniary aid."

Although Madison confined his analysis to terse statements shorn of detail, he constructed an analysis that enumerated significant relationships between two variables, government and religion. It was a controlled empirical inquiry on the Baconian model of concomitant variations, and its cumulative logic was powerful. When he moved, therefore, to the widest implications of the position with which he countered the Reverend Jasper Adams' charges, the ground had been prepared and assent followed. Madison found little warrant for the fear that if religion were left entirely to itself, it would demoralize society, weaken faith in authority, unleash individual and social excesses of a sinful and destructive sort. Having fully thought through his own position on religious and social freedom some half century earlier, he remained unimpressed by this argument. He commented that "the interference of government, in any form" might be more likely to increase than control the dangerous tendency, and that he trusted here, as he did in the purely political realm, the recurrence to reason as a brake on "excessive excitement." A world of experience and lifetime of shrewd but liberal thought went into his dry statement that "Great excitements are less apt to be permanent than to vibrate to the opposite extreme." At the end of the road, as at the beginning, he was unshaken in his judgment that there was *no* empirical ground for the claim that only religion could provide a basis for social morality and good government. Genuine religiousness in a people flourishes best without official support or regulation or compulsion of any sort from government.

In closing, Madison felt moved to express his admiration for the ability with which Reverend Adams had developed his position in his sermon. Further, Madison made one final observation of singular importance. He wrote: "I must admit . . . that it may not be easy, in every possible case, to trace the line of separation, between the rights of the religious and the civil authority, with such distinctness, as to avoid collisions and doubts on unessential points!" Nevertheless, the *principle* is unaffected—that there should be "an entire abstinence of the government from interference in any way whatever, beyond the necessity of preserving public order and protecting each sect against trespasses on its legal rights by others."

Madison's careful reaffirmation of the indispensable value of the principle of religious liberty stands in sharp contrast to the position taken by other eminent men of that day. Providentially, Dr. Adams had submitted his pamphlet to almost every important figure of the day, requesting comment thereon in each case. Among those who responded were Chief Justice John Marshall and Justice Joseph Story.[29] Neither one of these powerful jurists found fault with Dr. Adams' position.

John Marshall sent a suave reply: "The American population," he wrote, "is entirely Christian, and with us, Christianity and religion are identified. It would be strange indeed, if with such a people, our institutions did not presuppose Christianity. . . ." But Justice Story seized the occasion for an all-out endorsement, writing: "I have read it with uncommon satisfaction. I think its tone and spirit excellent. My own private judgment has long been (and every day's experience more and more confirms me in it) that government can not long exist without an alliance with religion to *some extent;* and that Christianity is indispensable to the true interests and solid foundations of free government" (italics added). This statement is the exact contrary of Madison's position, as we now know.

8

The counterpoint in these letters provides an accidental but illuminating dialogue between Madison and the two Supreme Court Justices. Their dialogue prompts a few reflections on the current controversies concerning religious freedom and government both inside and outside the Supreme Court.

First, if Madison's views and meanings are to be taken as a touchstone for the interpretation of the religious clause in the First Amendment, then it should by now be very clear that he intended a line of separation between religion and the government. This is the essence of what he meant by religious liberty. To this extent the judgment of Justice Story and those later Justices who have followed in his pattern of thought are forcing their own construction upon the law. Angry critics of the present-day Court, like Bishop James A. Pike, who claim that the Founding Fathers merely wanted to prohibit "laws respecting the recognition as an established church of any denomination, sect, or organized religious association" are unquestionably guilty of misrepresenting Madison's intent.

Second, as Madison was well aware, it is not always easy to draw the line. Part of the difficulty may arise from a conflict of rights. For example, the First Amendment provides that there shall be no establishment of religion but there shall be free exercise of religion, and free speech and press. In some cases one of these may conflict with another and therefore one must make a choice. Similarly, there may even be a conflict among religions, one prescribing practices that are proscribed by another, and one set of practices may also be prohibited by law. Human sacrifice and plural marriages are instances of such cases and therefore limit the religious freedom of some believers.

Third, the Supreme Court in certain of its rulings against Bible reading (as in the public schools of Pennsylvania, or in the Regents' prayer in the New York public schools), has been criticized for allegedly undermining morals and stunting or stifling the religious spirit of our people. Madison, in his constant rejection of religious establishment—whether of a single sect or across the board of the Christian religion—rejected the doctrine that there is a necessary connection between religion and morality. The significance of his life's work and one he explicitly set the highest value on, was to establish a free society on the basis of voluntary individual conscience and voluntary social morality, not on the basis of religious orthodoxy or dogma. In a word, he tried to establish a *secular* moral order as the American political system, and thought it might be good, perhaps even the best order ever devised.

Interestingly enough, the Supreme Court in the last twenty years has more and more come around to the Madisonian position on religious liberty. What we may consider the classic formulation of this view first appeared in a famous dissenting opinion on the parochial school bus case in 1947. The late Justice Rutledge wrote:

> No provision of the Constitution is more closely tied to or given content by its generating history than the religious clause of the First Amendment. It is at once the refined product and the terse summation of that history. The history includes not only Madison's authorship and the proceeding before the First Congress, but also the long and intensive struggle for religious freedom in America, more especially in Virginia, of which the Amendment was the direct culmination. . . . All the great instruments of the Virginia struggle for religious liberty thus became warp and woof of our constitutional tradition, not simply by the course of history, but by the common unifying force of Madison's life, thought and sponsorship.[30]

No doubt Madison would have been pleased with this tribute. But he knew and we know that we can pick our Supreme Court Justices. He would have been even more pleased with the fact that the minority judgment of 1947 has become the all but unanimous opinion of the Supreme Court in the Schempp Bible reading decision of 1963. The Education Bill of 1965, however, raised questions of religion and education and will undoubtedly give rise to a new series of "hard cases" before the Court in the coming years. The point is that this momentous shift in government aid to education would also have been a hard case for Madison! For the bill provided almost one billion dollars to be spent to strengthen public education in low-income areas, an action that amounted to a breakthrough because it was the first time in America's history that the federal government has granted substantial aid to public school education below the college level. But in addition, a comparatively small grant was provided for the purchase of books for school libraries for *all* schools in these same areas. The question then arises: does the provision of books for all schools, including parochial schools, outweigh as an evil the good that comes from the provision to support public education on so vast a scale? Here one can see a truly vexing conflict between two imperishable Madisonian ideals: to free the mind by providing the best possible education in the public schools and to give no aid, not even three pence, to support religion.

On the whole, it seems fair to say that Madison came as close to making an absolute of religious liberty as he ever did of any value in the bouquet traditionally available to men—and in Madison's words, men are not angels. He had other powerful principles and values; had he not, he would have been another being entirely, since the intelligent weighing of competing values, and the tireless use of intelligence to unravel intricate problems is characteristic of him, or nothing is. We shall explore some of these principles in the course of two more opportunities to look at the mind and character of "the great little Mr. Madison."

Chapter Two: Justice

Justice

INADEQUATE humanistic scholarship in America has done Madison a great disservice. I make this judgment sadly, and reserve from the generalization two recent works—the Hutchinson edition of the *Papers of James Madison,* now *in progress,* and Irving Brant's six-volume biography *Madison.* But it is difficult to escape the judgment that for over a century since his death, Madison has not received due recognition for his immense contributions to American history and thought.

Now, one reason we have been generally tendered an abstraction or a bitter caricature in place of the man has been partly the result of good intentions, partly accident, and only partly deliberate. Madison's early editors, for example, deleted a phrase from a youthful letter to William Bradford, his "old Nassovian Friend," dressing down some Tory pamphleteers. Madison was fuming about authors who write with "all the rage of impotence"—and here the delicacy of his editors made them delete the completion of the metaphor, which read "when passion seems to commit a rape on the understanding and engenders a little peevish snarling offspring." A less rational factor than such Victorian editing was American folk taste. Davy Crockett and Boone, frontier and flatboat mythology would come later; but even in Revolutionary days, Virginia leaders were meant to be tall—not only to be born to the saddle but to sit tall on it. Washington Irving's coinage of the phrase that Madison looked like a "withered little Applejohn" [1] established a caricature that kept him out of attractive books like Dixon Wector's *The Hero in America* and delayed the project of a memorial to him in the nation's capital to this very day.

On the more pompous level where historians and educators meet, one reflects on the irony of the fact that another attractive book which invariably appears these days on reading lists in American history courses of colleges and universities throughout the country, Richard Hofstadter's *The American Political Tradition and the Men Who Made It,* makes only the most perfunctory reference to Madison, in an opening chapter dutifully titled: "The Founding Fathers: An Age of Realism"—and those few references, I might add, support the kind of dogmatic selectivity that offers us a stuffy, conservative Mr. Madison, whose place in the history of freedom is nil.

Much of the trouble is traceable to Madison's fate with biographers in the nineteenth century. To make a long story short, let me simply mention that *the* big biography, William Cabell Rives' ponderous three volumes, made little impact although written by a man eminently qualified to deal with matters of domestic and foreign policy and who was himself a protégé of Jefferson and a neighbor and young friend of the Madisons. The narrative never reached beyond the point of the late 1790's, and the author died before he could complete the study. The second and third volumes were held up by the intervention of the Civil War; and since the first appeared on the eve of the war, and the other two in the wake of it, men were hardly in the mood during that tragic upheaval to wrestle with the intricate lessons of history and public policy that the slow-moving volumes contain. Curious fate! By the time men were able to read attentively again, it was Henry Adams, writing with marked animus against Madison, who offered a barbed portrait in his *History of the United States*—a portrait, incidentally, with no background or foreground, only the slice, as

Adams saw it, of Madison's official conduct as Secretary of State and as President. Thus the nineteenth century closed without a single full-length portrait and without a significant intellectual study of the man whose quiet gaze (or was it reproachful?) continued to peer out of the schoolbook pictures, which invariably bore the caption "Father of the Constitution."

And still the "pack of tricks" which Voltaire said was history played on. As part of the new social-scientific approach to history in America under the impetus of the Progressive movement and its passion for debunking the past, the "meaning" of the Constitution was viewed through economic determinist lenses, and Madison as its principal architect was seen in some murky way as the father of malign capitalism. I have no wish to enter upon the needlessly prolonged and myopic "Beard controversy" here. But to remove possible misinterpretation, let me say that the brilliance of Charles Beard's historical work, as a developing body of thought, should not, and I think cannot, be destroyed. After all, mind and spirit must not be counted as impedimenta in a profession like history! Nonetheless, progress—or advancing knowledge, even—brings about individual casualties. Beard's hypothesis, which soon became dogma, invited attention not to Madison, nor to his mind and complex political thought, nor to his subtle and elusive work as policy-maker and public servant, nor to his human traits and character, nor to his imperishable achievements—but rather to his supposed economic determinism, and to the Constitution as "an economic document," born of and reflecting property relationships of a sort allegedly beneficial to a "conservative" minority arrayed against a victimized "radical democratic" majority. I should now add that the persistence of the Beardian interpretation helps to explain the odd omission of a serious treatment of Madison from the book on the American political tradition mentioned above, a book which in a sense may be seen only as a more recent retracing of the figure in the carpet. Perhaps these tricks of history also may explain the irony in the current connotation of Madison Avenue.

However, amends are being made. In one or two cases, we have the paradox suggested by Benjamin Franklin's story of the man with one handsome and one deformed leg: most people stare at the deformed leg only; but an occasional few make themselves only see the shapely one! It remains the case, even now, that the future American Plutarch who could write his most glorious pages on Madison (so an admiring friend of Madison's once claimed) has *not* stepped forward. But this perhaps concerns me less than the lack of understanding of Madison's significance as a political thinker, which except for certain well-cut grooves, still remains the rule. Thus it is often the subject of loud complaint by pundits on American thought that there is no formal political classic—except the *Federalist* papers—in the whole body of American literature! One student [2] indeed finds *nothing* original about American political thinking; it is all a colossal borrowing of John Locke's ideas made prescriptive in the "American ethos." Another student who also began by lamenting the shocking absence of a single treatise on political philosophy in America, and who read very stern lessons to an amalgamated group known *to him* as "the Jeffersonian circle," for being what he saw as vulgar pragmatists or dogmatists, untouched by the higher truth of metaphysics, has come to make a virtue out of the fancied impoverishment and salutes American thinkers for, so to speak, *having no mind*—for trusting to "know how," to the intuitive instructions of the thick forests, the broad plains, and the non-ideological whisperings of pure experience.[3]

Following along these paths, it is sometimes

said that nowhere in American political writing can one find "a searching discussion of the nature of justice" [4]—the *Federalist* papers not excepted. The Founding Fathers presumably were good at contriving technicalities, means, but throw no light on the "first and most enduring values of organized society: justice, the general welfare, liberty."

2

I have therefore decided to explore the reasons why I think justice is the comprehensive goal of Madison's political thought and policies. I will readily grant, at the very outset, however, that if you approach the sizable body of Madison's writings with the mechanical reflex of one scanning an index (if only there were a reliable index, I might add!) looking at "J" for Justice, you will not find many entries; and on that kind of check one may decide that Madison had next to nothing to contribute on this age-old and persisting ideal. All the more must I grant that if one calls for a classic *treatise* labelled "On the Nature of Justice," the call will go unanswered.

Here, I am reminded of an odd bit of my own experience. When I first read Plato's *Republic* as a college student, I was mightily confused. The *Republic* has never yet been displaced as *the* seminal philosophical treatise on the nature of justice—its subtitle helping the literal-minded to see this well. Yet I recall my sense of having been horribly cheated, for where was the promised discussion? To be sure, in the introductory books Plato introduced Cephalus, the old man, who proposed that justice be considered giving each man his due; but he was summarily dispatched by Socrates who queried, "Yes, but what *is* his due?" At this hint of trouble, Cephalus made polite noises, inviting his guests to remain, dine, etc., and withdrew to propitiate the gods. Then Plato introduced Thrasymachus and followers, the angry young men of Athens, who with equal promptness pronounced that justice was merely "the interest of the stronger"—the parent theory of what goes by the name of "might makes right." Socrates clearly disapproved, although he said little except that even a band of thieves required some sense of internal loyalty and justice to be a *successful* band of thieves. At length Socrates was smoked out (just as he wanted to be) and proceeded to construct for his listeners the famous outline of the Republic, the society—perhaps only to be seen in the stars and the sky—that would be created when (or if) a philosopher became king. Rubbing the slate clean, Socrates, speaking for the philosopher-king, divided society into three classes: king or ruler; auxiliaries; and workers, or producers. To each was assigned a special virtue; wisdom for the King, courage for the guardians, temperance or moderation for the producers. And justice? *That*, says Socrates, is the result, the proper functioning of the three classes. Justice is that which makes the harmony of the whole state; it is the organizing principle of the state but not otherwise describable than in terms of the principle that each class (presumably also each member of the class) is busily doing what it or he ought to be doing. It was only on my second and successive readings that I saw what Plato meant by justice and learned that *his* implied concept of a just state was one where people were rigidly yoked to a pre-formed function, and each class was subservient to "the good of the whole" as decreed by the philosopher–king—and then I knew it could not be mine.

Let us return now to Madison and his thought on justice. We have seen that Madison attached peculiar significance to his doctrine of religious liberty. The core of that doctrine is that there should be no connection between government and religion, and that to the extent that a political order can maintain this ideal, it is—to that extent—a free society, and as free, good. It is also true that there is a vital connection made in Madison's theory between religious liberty and his more general theory of political liberty. Two elements should be noted. One element in Madison's notion of religious liberty has to do with a person's beliefs, with his personal conscience—the element that Madison, in the language drawn from social compact and natural rights theory, calls "unalienable." If one prefers, it might be stated as the view that man's reason and conscience come from the hands of God. But there is a second element that is clearly social and belongs to civil society. It is the element that states that political arrangements should be so ordered as to recognize, to the greatest extent possible, the unalienable rights of conscience. The recognition of the unalienability of man's right to think and choose and judge is at the heart of his theory that there must not be cognizance of religion by government.

Thus Madison's notion of religious liberty contains the claim that the government should treat each person as a person (not merely a means), that each person's claim to this fundamental moral concern on the part of government is *equal.* It is an equal claim, without preference to what his religious beliefs are or what the convictions of his conscience are. These equal claims are in full force as prohibitions on the power of government unless and until they ride roughshod over the beliefs of others or create injuries to others or generally violate the rules of order, disturbing the public peace. The second element of religious liberty, demanding equal treatment under government, even equal treatment for disturbances ruled in advance to be punishable, moves beyond the purely personal right and embraces the relationships that *should* exist among persons if a free society is to exist. *The concern with persons on the grounds of equality with respect to their moral and political existence is the essence of justice.* From this point of view a just society is based on the consent of the people, the persons who comprise that society. And a society is more just to the extent that it promotes the conditions toward equal treatment while recognizing the different needs and characteristics and abilities of people who, while alike in being the object of equal concern, are diverse in an infinitude of other ways.

For Madison, what we today call a democratic government and he called a republican form of government, is the best form men can devise to realize the ideal of justice. In these terms, the problems of justice are the most basic problems with which the founding fathers were preoccupied—as Madison himself suggested when he defined his political contribution in terms of his devotion to "the cause of liberty."

When we see justice in these terms, we are able to account for the misunderstanding that there is no philosophy of justice in the American Enlightenment, and in Madison. For the misunderstanding arises from the presupposition that only formal and overt analysis of the concept in general moral and historical terms constitutes an inquiry into the nature of justice. Neither Madison nor other Enlightened statesmen of the day were "uninterested in theory"; they were not rebels against theory, nor devotees of an untutored involvement in experience. They were inquiring into what the term "*government based on consent*" really might mean, apart from its honorific status in formal political treatises. They were searching, so to speak, for an operational definition of *consent*, of *justice*, of *freedom*—and they put their thought to elaborating the durable and workable political means which would create a government of laws, not of men, under conditions of greater freedom and self-fulfillment than had been attained in the brightest eras of human history.

3

This approach to the great questions of politics was typically an Enlightenment enterprise, an experiment on Baconian lines, where the purpose of systematic reflection was to improve the condition of man by new inventions. The American state constitutions were such experiments, carefully formulated by theoretical discussions and plans in advance, and sharpened under the live debate and adjudication of competing, but rationally defended, interests—both inside and outside the legislative chambers. But the greatest of these experiments was indeed the Federal Constitution. Madison knew this to the hilt. He once told Edward Coles that the work of reporting the debates in the Convention—in addition to his heavy responsibilities in debate, committee, and outside discussion with other members—nearly killed him. We know, of course, that he lived a half century after that, outliving all other members of the Convention. No doubt the reward of virtue! But even in his will, Madison, providing for the publication of his Notes on the debates in the Federal Convention, continued to believe that something worth all one could give was represented in them. He wrote:

> Considering the peculiarity and magnitude of the occasion which produced the convention at Philadelphia in 1787, the Characters who composed it, the Constitution which resulted from their deliberation, its effects during a trial of so many years on the prosperity of the people living under it, and the interest it has inspired among the friends of free Government, it is not an unreasonable inference that a careful and extended report of the proceedings and discussions of that body, which were with closed doors, by a member who was constant in his attendance, will be particularly gratifying to the people of the United States, and to all who take an interest in the progress of political science and the cause of true liberty.[5]

4

Madison was often called the master-builder of this new model of free government. But Madison himself did not accept the sweeping compliment that was often tendered to him as "the father of the Constitution." He had written crisply on this very matter to an admirer:

> You give me a credit to which I have no claim, in calling me "*the* writer of the Constitution of the United States." This was not, like the fabled Goddess of Wisdom, the offspring of a single brain. It ought to be regarded as the work of many heads & many hands.[6]

Indeed, many of the members of the Convention possessed political genius and played their part in the shaping of the instrument. But Madison outdistanced all the other delegates by his initial preparation and by his sustained and ubiquitous efforts in the Convention. He came to the Convention after an intensive scholarly preparation. We have seen that he had read carefully on the subject of government, and that his attendance in Princeton at the lectures of President John Witherspoon and his very close association with him in a friendly tutorial relationship, had made the ideas of the Scottish common sense philosophers, and of their prime philosophical challenger, David Hume, familiar intellectual territory for him. Years before the Convention, he had initiated a campaign to bolster up the impotent Confederation by obtaining for Congress a general and permanent power to regulate the commerce of the United States, knowing that nothing short of drafting a new constitution would suffice. In 1786 he joined with Alexander Hamilton in like-minded co-operation in the Annapolis Convention, although their political views would diverge sharply when the Convention actually came about. They managed to extract from that sparsely attended deputation a radical measure couched in deliberately mild terms—an address to Congress and the States, written by Hamilton, recommending the calling of another convention, with more power vested in the deputies, to devise provisions "to render the constitution of the federal government adequate to the exigencies of the Union."

In the highly interesting intervening period between Annapolis in the fall of 1786, and the Federal Convention in Philadelphia, Madison found the time, despite his pressing political activities, to re-educate himself in the literature of political history and ancient and distinctly modern political thought. Through the friendship of Jefferson, Madison deliberately procured for himself a kind of five-foot shelf of books on the history of natural law, political history, economics, and science, ancient and modern confederacies, and the social philosophy of the Enlightenment, including the Baconian-inspired thirty-seven-volume set of the *Encyclopédie Methodique,* the up-to-date summa of knowledge. The two principal directors of the *Encyclopédie,* Denis Diderot and Jean d'Alembert, and many of its contributing *philosophes,* were devotees of the scientific humanism of Francis Bacon, and no reader could miss the pervasive evidence in that great work of Bacon's distinctive faith in the power of science and technology to advance and improve the daily lot of man. It is noteworthy that Bacon's *Advancement of Learning* served as the acknowledged model for the *Encyclopédie.*

Two influential papers of Madison's justify his time spent with books before the Federal Convention opened. The first was a set of analytical notes on ancient and modern confederacies,[7] in which Madison briefly described and commented on salient features of the organization of each—such as the conditions of representation for member states or cities, the stipulations regarding financial levies or taxes, the scope and specific powers of the general authority, and the range of autonomous government retained by the member states. Madison was obviously interested in two questions: in virtue of exactly *what* had the confederated powers flourished, and what "vices" of their constitutions had enfeebled them or caused them either to dissolve or to be overthrown? These questions he put to "history," in order to prepare himself to conceive an improved "constitution" for a modern confederacy, one that would not be subject to the "vices" he had pinpointed in the confederacies of the past. He was also pondering how to enhance features of organization that had proven to be valuable, or that seemed to Madison promising, from the point of view of republican ideals. One should note that Madison's principal sources of information and critical comment in these notes were the two outstanding compilations of the French Enlightenment: the *Encyclopédie;* and even more extensively, the thirteen-volume *Code de L'Humanité*, a recently published work on "universal, natural, civil and political law,"[8] which Madison had requested Jefferson to purchase for him in Paris in April 1785.

The upshot of Madison's diagnosis of the Lycian, Amphictyonic, Achaean, Helvetic, Belgic, and Germanic confederacies reverted usually to the theme that the decisive fault lay in one or another form of insufficient power in the general authority over the member states, or in the unjust treatment of the less powerful by the more powerful members of the confederacy. Both harmony (internal peace) and the power to produce that harmony and survive as a defensive unit against hostile external forces are basic criteria in the appraisal of ancient and modern confederacies. Not only Madison's scholarly sources, but assuredly Madison himself, may be read to mean that these criteria bear upon future attempts as well. They are, in short, the universal generalizations for successful patterns of confederation.

The second paper of Madison's came just a month before the Constitutional Convention opened. It was a trenchant critique, based upon his own (fully authoritative!) experience, of the "Vices of the Political System of the United States."[9] Although Madison had no need to pause for annotation in this brief review of the inadequacies of harmony and energy under the governance of the Articles of Confederation, his analysis of events and "vices" bore evidence of the clarity induced by his prior study and reflection on the lessons of political history. Without doubt, this paper is the more consequential one, since it contained many of Madison's seminal political ideas on a federal republic, including his distinctive emphasis on the value of an *extensive republic*.[10] While the first paper on the ancient and modern confederacies might be considered Madison's necessary worksheets, the second, on the weakness of the confederacy in the United States, had the creative vigor and coherence of a master.

The two papers together—the worksheets and the position paper—testify to Madison's *formal* preparation for the coming Convention. Yet, the real source of his strength, as he was about to enter the Convention, lay in the decade and more of his political experience in the affairs of Virginia and the Continent. Madison had become wise the hard way, in his role as a "representative" and as a legislative draftsman wrestling with the multitudinous aspects of politics in an era of revolutionary upheaval and new-made independence. In his dozen years of political activity from '75 to '87, Madison had acquired an enviable reputation for sagacity as a political leader because of his efforts to promote liberal legislation in Virginia and to forward a continentalist outlook in place of the more habitual, shortsighted, and narrow state loyalties.

When Madison arrived early with the Virginia delegation to the Constitutional Convention (they were the first to settle in, better prepared than any other for the protracted struggle of wits), he masterminded the "Virginia Plan" which Governor Randolph presented. This constitutional sketch proposed not a "stronger" Confederacy, as is so often misleadingly said, but a federated Republic with effective powers to govern the people directly, without depending upon the permissions and refusals of thirteen sovereign, independent states in matters claimed for the general authority. Madison's theory of an improved and viable, modern federalism was his unique contribution to the republic defined in the Constitution, and one he found it necessary to expound again and again.

Madison was entirely convinced that the American political system, with its innovations, created an emergent new level in political science—by which he meant political knowledge of a testable kind. He had this in mind when he asserted, as he often did, that that government was best which was least imperfect; and that "The compound Government of the United States is without a model, and to be explained by itself, not by similitudes or analogies." [11]

It was a Republic, yet not like other republics; a federal republic, but not like other confederacies; a national government, although not purely national; a large, a very extensive republic, intended for future growth, quite unlike other large states in the past that had been despotisms.[12]

The federal constitution had been created by men who knew "the power of reason" and understood "the lessons of experience." Step by step, in a gruelling four months that followed upon more than a decade of political experimentation, the men who framed the Constitution devised a system that combined, as Madison said, the theoretic freedom of a small community, with the practical advantages of a great one. All previous governments, he thought, had been unacceptable in terms of justice, for they tended either to despotism or to anarchy. The American version of federalism lifted the threat of both of these systems of human bondage. The concurrent system, the state governments, which prevented the federal government from becoming despotic, and the federal government, which made the supreme law of the land in the functions entrusted to it, kept the states from that fatal insubordination that spelled anarchy and kept them from that fatal dwarfing that spelled consolidation.

After the pressures of the Federal Convention came the rush deadlines of the essays for Madison's share of the *Federalist*. In the case of the *Federalist*, hailed throughout the world as the undisputed "classic" of American political theory, one sometimes wonders whether Mark

Twain's definition is in force. "A classic," the master asserted, "is something that everybody wants to have read and nobody wants to read." At any rate, there seems to be very little evidence that the academicians and the critics have probed the pages of the "classic" they applaud. For the prevailing "treatment" concentrates on a few papers only—in Madison's case almost entirely on the Tenth *Federalist*. This preoccupation has had consequences that bear on our interpretation.

It encourages an unnatural emphasis upon property interests. It is a fact that this kind of dominant preoccupation permitted Charles Beard to construct an ideological justification for his interpretation of the whole framing (in the pejorative sense, often!) of the Constitution. Before going further, must we bother to say that the economic interpretation of history is a misleading and false description of Madison's aims in his constitutional masterplan? For one certainly should *not* have to choose between "abstract" generalizations, purely moral concerns, and *real concrete* economic interests! Was Madison subserving property? Or was he attempting to provide more equal opportunity for all interests to gain a hearing at the bar of a just legal system? The clue to this as his overriding interest is derivable from the thought underlying Madison's strong views on religious liberty. There, it will be recalled, Madison repeatedly stressed the multiple and diverse sects, indicating that each had a claim to be considered by just public policy. *All* sects would profit by religious freedom in the sense that none need fear annihilation at the hands of an overextended and presumptuous religious monopoly or establishment. The fact is, as Gaillard Hunt pointed out, Madison often quoted approvingly Voltaire's aphorism: "If one religion only were allowed in England, the government would possibly become arbitrary; if there were but two, the people would cut each other's throats; but as there are such a multitude, they all live happy and in peace."[13] (It is worth notice that this statement of Voltaire's comes from his article on "Tolerance" in the *Philosophical Dictionary,* another of the books which Jefferson purchased for Madison in Paris.) Multiplicity of interests as the road to tolerance, and *beyond* to freedom, is the principle Madison develops in his philosophy of an extensive republic.

For Madison the great virtue of a republic is to provide that liberty which permits factions to breathe and to provide those internal and external limits on destructive license, which encourage reasonable compromise of the multiple conflicting interests. He not only recognizes diversity but welcomes it, and provides for the kind of order that emerges from compromise and reciprocal controls. He is much concerned on all important questions with what he prudently calls "requisite power" and energy in government, but he invariably joins these necessary means with their proper ends—liberty, justice, and the rights of the people.

Fortunately, we need not rest on inference from other contexts. I refer to Madison's *Federalist* 51, which is, from first to last, an essay on the character of federalism as a just political system. It opens with the question: how can we maintain the Constitution's provisions for a limited government, of separated powers—how maintain them in practice, since practice is notoriously capable of twisting and changing the constitutional system? Number 51 provides Madison's answer on what to rely on, and his proposal is "by so contriving the interior structure of the government that its several constituent parts may, by their mutual relations, be the means of keeping each other in their proper places." [14]

The first principle is the preservation of liberty. For this object, separate and distinct powers of government are specified in the Constitution. A *concentration* of the several powers of government in the same department, the same hands, sets up a tyranny, not a limited constitutional government under which liberty may be preserved.

The best security against a "gradual concentration" of power in the same department consists in providing each limited department of government with fortification against attack. The strategy, as Madison says, is that "ambition must be made to counteract ambition. The interest of the man must be connected with the constitutional rights of the place." It is then that he remarks, in a classic passage: "It may be a reflection on human nature, that such devices should be necessary to control the abuses of government. But what is government itself, but the greatest of all reflections on human nature? If men were angels, no government would be necessary. If angels were to govern men, neither external nor internal controls on government would be necessary."[15] This admirably compressed statement is normally used to tip off more or less literary explications of the inherent weakness, viciousness, etc., of human nature, and Madison's "pessimism" or "realism" about human beings. All very well, save that it sends us on a false chase and we lose the quarry. For what Madison immediately adds is that "In framing a government which is to be administered by men over men, the great difficulty lies in this: you must first enable the government to control the governed; and in the next place oblige it to control itself. A dependence on the people is, no doubt, the primary control on the government, but experience has taught mankind the necessity of auxiliary precautions."

In short, the realism about human nature applies equally to the whole people, the majority of the people, any minority faction, and any select groups of short-term or long-term officials of government (representatives in Congress, for example, and members of the judiciary). Since the trail of the human serpent is upon us all—governors and governed alike—justice will not come by way of simple resort to "the people," nor by way of simple majority rule, nor by simple elite rule, nor by simple one-man or dictatorship rule. Needless to say, it will never come by way of military rule. The *only* policy to overcome the partial and self-regarding impulses that may lead any and all of us astray is that of "supplying, by opposite and rival interests, the defect of better motives"—a policy, says Madison, "that might be traced through the whole system of human affairs, private as well as public." [16] This clearly is a universal generalization about human conduct whether in the home, the church, the school, the marketplace, or the highest places of government. "Divide and rule" Madison once phrased it—check and balance so that "the private interest of every individual may be a sentinel over the public rights." These are "the inventions of prudence," and they operate to promote the public rights.[17]

How do these general observations about the nature of government and the nature of the men who are the governed apply to the American federal system? Madison points out that "the compound republic of America" provides "a double security . . . to the rights of the people. The different governments (federal and state) will control each other, at the same time that each will be controlled by itself." A federal republic is in this sense more likely to be a just government (protecting the public rights) than is a single republic, as a double rope walk over a mountain chasm is likely to be more reliable than a single rope. (Yet, true, both remain to some irreducible extent precarious, for the chasm is always there and the foot may slide.) Madison underlines the importance in a republic of guarding against oppression from both quarters —not only from the rulers over the ruled, but "from one part of the society against the injustice of the other part." [18]

A free society, as he has amply shown in all his preceding writings, is composed of a multitude of interests, an undetermined number of factions, "in different classes of citizens." Danger of oppression exists when the majority, united by a common interest, negate the rights of a minority. There is majority tyranny (thus he anticipated the precise problem that Tocqueville half a century later, would make central to the democratic civilization). A republic alone *need* worry about majority tyranny, since other forms (aristocratic or monarchial, despotic or paternalistic) do not derive from and clear the way for majority rule and thus *their* problems are typically the tyranny of the minority, not the majority. Since the minority is the vulnerable sector in a majoritarian society, there are only two methods of preventing majority tyranny. One method is to create a will in the community independent of the majority—but this may deliver majority and all but a handful of the original minority alike into the hands of exploitative, independent rulers. Madison is not tempted by this alternative.

The second and remaining remedy is to comprehend in the society "so many separate descriptions of citizens as will render an unjust combination of a majority of the whole very improbable, if not impracticable." He does not promise, note, an absolute or surefire remedy; the precarious gulf yawns below; but this systematic and strongly fibered bridge may do it. And this second method is exemplified in the federal republic of the United States. All authority there derives from and depends on the society; but the society is not a totalitarian mass, but a *multiverse*. It is "broken into so many parts interests and class of citizens, that the rights of individuals or of the minority will be in little danger from interested combinations of the majority." Equal liberty is incompatible with simple majoritarian democracy! If men seriously ask for equality and seriously care about liberty they will see that it takes them to a free government where "the security for civil rights must be the same as that of religious rights. It consists in the one case in the multiplicity of interests, and in the other in the multiplicity of sects." [19]

Moreover, the degree of security in both cases will depend on the number of interests and sects —the more, the more just the society is likely to be. Thus, a populous society richly diversified, and covering a big extent of country is likely to be governable as a free, federal republic more than any small state league is. Only then does Madison make his statement, summing up his plea for the protection of public rights through an extensive federal republic: "Justice is the end of government. It is the end of civil society. It ever has and ever will be pursued until it is obtained, or until liberty be lost in the pursuit." [20]

In a brief, brilliant passage Madison then compares the state of nature, where even the stronger individuals agree to enter government, thus yielding some of their natural strength, but gaining greater security for themselves as also for the naturally weak; so in an unjust society where majority factions prey upon minority rights, the resulting anarchy will in time make those very factions sue for the conditions of a just society. What he has in mind is suggested by the final comparison between Rhode Island, if left to herself, outside the federal republic, and the "extended republic of the United States." The former would suffer from such oppression by the local majorities that the cry for reform by means of a just and more equal system would soon come from within the majority sector itself; while the extensive Republic with all its "great variety of interests, parties and sects" could not form a coalition of a majority of the whole society unless it did so on the principles "of justice and the general good." It is clear that a coalition of the majority for justice and the general good is possible and desirable; but on the minimal rule used by prudence, precautions are taken to protect each of the diverse interests in a nonpreferential system of equal concern and justice. "The larger society, provided it lie within a practical sphere, the more duly capable it will be of self-government. And happily for the republican cause, the practicable sphere may be carried to a very great extent, by a judicious modification and mixture of the federal principle." [21]

5

In concentrating on *Federalist* 51 instead of 10, I have not dealt with another important phase of the *Federalist* papers. Although they are normally treated as a unity, there is in fact a split personality within the *Federalist* papers.[22] What is involved here is the perception of a serious theoretical conflict between two substantially different views of the federal system. One view looks to the unity and energy the system establishes. This is the Hamiltonian position. The other view looks to the extensive republic which is achieved by the unique complex of diverse interests which, under the proposed system, recognize majority rights while protecting the rights of the minority. This is the Madisonian position, which conjoins liberty and justice to "the requisite powers" of government. I have elaborated these points elsewhere, where I tried to indicate certain difficulties in Hamilton's theory and personality which raise susbtantial problems about the direction and magnitude of his contribution.[23] All I need indicate now is that he did not believe in or support any serious measures designed to promote the sovereignty of the people, and that his central concern was the strength and energy of the national government. For this reason, alone, if no other, we can see the distinctive quality of Madison's contribution. He actively worked in and undertook leadership in the Convention, while Hamilton retired from the battle when his elitist views met no favor. Hamilton then joined with Madison on the *Federalist* papers because he saw the Constitution as the only attainable instrument to push towards a stronger national government, and not primarily because it promoted a more just liberal order.

The idea of a federal republic was the distinctive creation and development of Madison. In the work that followed upon the convention, and in the writing of the *Federalist,* Madison redoubled his service to the cause of the Constitution. One cannot emphasize too strongly the importance of the debates in the Virginia Convention of 1788, for the survival of the plan for a just yet free society. One must take account of them to indicate Madison's role in history. The massed brilliance of the Virginia delegation to the Constitutional Convention, exceeding that of any other state, made the acceptance or rejection by Virginia of crucial importance. If the Constitution had been condemned by the state that had initiated the call for a Convention (and moved by Madison), and that had sent, with other illustrious men, George Washington to preside over its deliberations, Governor Edmund Randolph to head the delegation, James Madison to create the initial major plan and untie the Gordian knots put to the Convention by the tangle of conflicting interests—if condemned by the state that had pioneered its cause and that enjoyed an inevitable prominence from its great size, wealth, and illustrious past, the Constitution would have collapsed as a live plan, no matter how many states had ratified, no matter even if New York had ratified—an assumption so unlikely that it must be entertained for courteous reasons only.

In the Virginia Convention, Madison of course led the Federalist group, and Patrick Henry the anti-Federalists. Pitted against the unmatchable oratory of Henry, Madison had the handicap of a weak voice and the self-restraint to refuse those emotive appeals that often carry the day.

Two interesting contemporary estimates of Madison's role in achieving ratification in Virginia were made by men who were by no means always to be found in his political corner. The first is John Marshall's remark that if eloquence include the art of "persuasion by conviction, Mr. Madison was the most eloquent man I ever heard." [24] A more circumstantial (and more vivid) account unexpectedly occurs in the course of the eulogy pronounced on Madison by his neighbor and longtime family friend, James Barbour, former Governor of Virginia, United States Senator, and a Whig who was a close associate of John Quincy Adams.[25]

"In striking contrast to Henry," he wrote, Madison was "modest even to bashfulness"; instead of "the strong and melodious voice of Henry, his was inconveniently feeble, so that when he rose to speak, the members, lest they should lose a word, were accustomed to gather around him. He used little or no gesture; his style of speaking was pure and simple, and without ornament. Yet, modestly confiding in his own vast resources, and strong in the conviction of the righteousness of his cause, day after day, for six weeks, he continued to wrestle successfully with his gigantic opponent. To his [Henry's] eloquence he opposed a calm appeal to the understanding, sustained by references to the experience of the past, and more especially that furnished by the free states of antiquity . . . furnishing, now, beacons by which we should profit, demonstrating with the clearness of a sunbeam, the necessity of a change in the federal Government. . . . These efforts were the more successful on account of his high character for disinterested ends, awarded him alike by friend and foe—I mean political foe, for private he had none; so that his words fell upon his audience like the response of an ancient oracle—adored for its truth and wisdom. In fine, the good genius of his country was in him personified. . . ." To this tribute, Barbour added another piece of significant comment: "The conflict between these giants and their auxiliaries was enacted before an audience to which every quarter of the Union had contributed some of its most distinguished citizens; and was so full of interest that, to enjoy it, industry gave up its pursuits and dissipation forbore its indulgences." [26] Apparently, the "oracle" was listened to by a thronged audience of spectators and the give-and-take of ideas about the Constitution was brought home to the People on the spot.

6

At this point, it may be useful to summarize and comment briefly on the significance of Madison's efforts to frame a constitution. First, we have seen that justice is that ideal of the political order which is concerned with the distribution of rights to persons on the basis of their equality before the law, both in its formulation and its application. Furthermore, it is an ideal that in practice is approximated more or less, so that one discriminates among states, or between periods within a given state, by the degree to which the ideal is realized.

Second, what is specifically American is the continuous attempt to frame constitutions which are guided by this ideal of justice. Where much of political philosophy has been concerned with developing and arguing about the implications of this ideal, the American experience was one marked by the concern with framing operating instruments of government to realize it. This continuous concern to realize consent by the people is illustrated not only by the provisions of the various state constitutions, conceived and referred to as "experiments," but also by the debates and discussions about those constitutions. What is specifically novel, "without analogy" to previous history, are two elements in the framing of the Federal Constitution. One element is the degree to which previous history of governments and their constitutions were critically reviewed and appraised. The other element was the mechanism by which this appraisal was subject to consent or dissent by the means of a specially constituted assembly convened to consider framing a constitution, and followed by the debates on ratifying the proferred constitution. Here we see an intellectual component involving careful discussion, and criticism of historical examples and institutional recommendations by way of constitutional provisions. These are disciplined intellectual exercises, guided by explicit problems and concerns, and constitute a necessary element of any experimental theory.

Third, Madison played a leading and commanding role in every phase of the experimental process. He made it his business to study systematically the history of all governments, the general laws that might be said to frame a constitution for those governments, and the philosophical inquiries on just government. He learned by experience in his specific political work as a member of the Virginia Assembly and the Continental Congress. He was indefatigable and resourceful in drafting and discussing proposals. All this explains his effort to retain the most detailed record of the debates in the Convention, because of his awareness of the historical uniqueness and importance of the process and content of the deliberations.

Fourth, there was Madison's strategy. It involved judgment on what he should be silent about—and not actively propose. He was trying to concretize what he felt could be achieved for a more just state than previously existed and the most just state that could be made acceptable under his appraisal of what the complex conditions permitted. On the positive side, this involved the fundamental notion of the Federal idea which rested both the state and federal governments on the consent of the people, rather than making the federal government a creature of the states.

But on the negative side was the failure to

advance *full* suffrage. In this I include the failure of equal suffrage to those who may not have had the property qualifications; the rejection of persons on account of race or color; and the rejection of persons on account of sex. This last qualification of sex even Jefferson ignored in the most advanced thinking of that day. The point is that there are degrees of justice and that the most just under given conditions may be insufficient and inadequate under other conditions. So that when we talk of the "undemocratic" features of the Constitution, we must never forget that most of those criticisms are explicitly made for the discriminations of the first two kinds and almost never made about the last kind! In effect, I am reverting to what I have called Madison's attitude of strategic compromise. One cannot get everything at once. We are involved in appraising what is do-able on the one hand, and the set of priorities on the other hand. Now, we ought to appraise a reform program in terms of whether the reform moves to more just conditions than existed prior to the institution of the reform and whether it selects more important rather than less important issues.

Finally, on all of these grounds, we must judge Madison achieved greatness. We see that he was, in truth, the master-builder of the Constitution. Unfortunately, the glacial title "Father of the Constitution" functions more often as a thought-stopper than as a crystallization of the imaginative and manifold measures and thought Madison took in forwarding his masterplan for a just political order.

Today, when men prefer to talk about myths rather than moral and political principles, when "puncturing a myth" is taken as the badge of the skilled intellectual toreador, the work of Madison in framing the Constitution is often approached with a singular lack of understanding. Certainly the contemporary mind falls short of the insight manifested by a forgotten Whig senator, in a forgotten speech—I refer to the speech made by Asher Robbins of Rhode Island as he rose on February 18, 1837 to advocate passage of the resolution to purchase and publish Madison's papers. A half-century had passed since the formation of the Constitution and the Senator, who had been a college tutor after his graduation from Yale, had subsequently studied and practiced law, and had already served in the U.S. Senate for a dozen years. In this speech, Senator Robbins developed a powerful comparison between the work of James Madison and Francis Bacon's epoch-making treatise, the

Novum Organum. He spoke then as a man of some learning, but unmistakably also as a man of conviction.

Bacon, he asserted, "produced that revolution in analytics, which has occasioned the immense superiority of the moderns over the ancients in the knowledge of Nature, and in the improvement of the condition of human life—the fruit of that knowledge." With Bacon, he added, it was a mere theory, although a theory he fondly cherished, and confidently believed would be prolific of the most magnificent results. "And rightly so, for this [*Novum*] *Organum* has been the beacon-light of mankind to guide him to true philosophy, and to the improvement of his physical condition." Just so, he said, would Madison's notes on the Federal Convention become the "beacon-light to guide man to the true science of free government, and to the improvement of his political condition"—*the science of free government*. He observed that it was the most difficult of all the sciences, but far and away "the most important to mankind; of all, the slowest in growth, the latest in maturity." Robbins envisaged the exceptional difficulties of creating a free government, and then commented that this science, unlike others, could *not* create a perfect model applicable everywhere.

The model of a free government, he pointed out, "though the principles are the same everywhere, the form varies as the circumstances vary, of the people by whom it is established; to which circumstances it must always be adjusted and made to conform." Looking back to the origin of the American constitutional system, he judged that the fact that the difficulties were overcome at all appeared to him "little less than a prodigy."

Most effective was the climax of his speech. "Here were a people" he continued, "spread and spreading over a vast territory, stretching and to stretch almost from the rising to the setting sun—this scattered and countless multitude were to be ruled in freedom as one people and by the popular will—that will was to be uncontrolled in itself, and controlling everything. Such an achievement the most enlightened friends of freedom and human rights, in all countries, and in all ages, had deemed to be morally and physically impossible. Besides, here were thirteen States, and all the other States to be formed out of that vast territory, without being destroyed as States, to be so combined as to form, in the general aspect, but one simple government, with all the unity and energy . . . for all the purposes of peace and war. Such an achievement, often before, and under much more favorable circumstances, because upon a much more limited scale, had been attempted, but never before accomplished; as is but too well attested by the histories and the destinies of all the confederacies that before . . . existed on the earth." In sum, Senator Robbins located the novelty of the American model of free government in its federalism—its divided sovereignty—a principle "unexplored and unknown before . . . our confederate and national republic." He paid tribute to Madison for his theory of Federalism and for the commanding role he played in engineering this system from idea to reality.[27]

7

Here again, as in the case of the First Amendment, we are not simply dealing with dead history or an abstract formula. On the contrary, the issues of federalism today are very much alive, not only here, in these United States, but in the world. Its vitality in this country is evidenced by the "great debate" now current on the fiscal aspects of federalism, the best way to meet the needs of states and local governments while Federal revenues rise. Let me briefly outline this issue, since it gives reality to the claim of the current vitality of the Federalist idea.

Under our federal system, state and local governments have the responsibility for providing their citizens with many of the most important ingredients of civilized life. Citizens of the United States depend on their state and local governments for the education of their children, the safety of their water, the protection of their persons and property from fire and crime, and many other essential services. Improvement in the quality of these services—especially health and education—is an important part of what we mean by a "rising standard of living."

However, state and local governments by themselves do not have the resources necessary to meet the demands placed on them for improving and expanding these essential public services.

In the past, the national need for state-local services in excess of state-local resources has been met by federal grants-in-aid for particular purposes. These specific federal grants have been of considerable help in relieving state-local fiscal burdens. Nevertheless, the states have long been pressing for a more general and far-reaching solution to their resource needs—the transfer to them from the federal government of major revenue sources. Such transfers would help solve the basic difficulties the states have in meeting the needs of their citizens in areas of clear state-local responsibility, without transferring control of these areas or decisions on spending priorities to the federal government.

Though sympathetic to state-local fiscal problems, the federal government up to now has found its own responsibilities for defense, foreign affairs, and other functions too heavy to permit turning major revenue sources over to the states for general purposes. Once the pressure for increased expenditures on account of Vietnam has abated, it would seem that other expenditures in areas of federal responsibility will not rise as rapidly as federal revenues at present tax rates. This prospect provides the opportunity for a more general and permanent solution to the state-local fiscal crisis than has been possible up to now.

Seen in this light, the idea of federalism still remains a principle of shared sovereignty, responsive and responsible to the needs and will of the people in whom ultimate sovereignty resides. As a careful student of this subject, Governor Nelson Rockefeller said in his Godkin Lectures, *The Future of Federalism:*

> The Federal idea, like the whole American experience, is a political adventure. It is no static thing, no dead definition, no dogmatic proclamation. Old as it is in our history, its secret strength is that it forever summons a free people to learn and try the new.
>
> It requires us, I believe, to imitate its authors in only one respect: to be, like them, unchained to the past and unfearful of the future, to be—in our time as they were in theirs—political pioneers.[28]

I have nothing further to add, except that when Madison pioneered our course for a just society he wore no blindfold over his eyes!

Chapter Three: Union

Union

THERE is an old Spanish proverb in which I believe—"Take what you want," said God. "Take it, and pay for it." The history of ideas and human ideals is not exempt from this warning. Men who value freedom and justice, attempt, if they are sincere and courageous, to establish them on a better footing than they had before. But suppose they succeed? They have then successfully established more freedom and more justice and like others who "ordain and establish" anything, from a mere innovation in a college curriculum to the establishment of a free, federated Republic, they have a stake *to protect*. No longer free in the sovereign choice of how to crush infamy, once they have taken up their weapons, they are committed. In the moment of creation for ideal ends the future presses, threatening a not-long deferred bill of payment. The final chapter meets Madison on this ground.

Union

1

Successful beyond rightful expectation, champion of many of the great reforms that constitute the American experiment, Madison retired from his second term as President accompanied by an unusual outburst of gratitude throughout the nation. As he had seen many years before, the art of free society was the most demanding art men (who were *not* angels) would ever take under wing. What had guided him thus far and would see him through to the end was the principle that wherever the preponderant power in society was lodged, *there* was the prime danger of abuse. Through forty years of creative statesmanship he had possessed the sharp judgment to detect the preponderant power no matter what mask it wore. And, unfailingly, when Madison felt the abuse of power, and was sure of the gravity of the abuse, he fought. So it was that he had come through his long career, from young Virginia revolutionary to the close of his second term in office on March 4, 1817, surviving the normal threats of annihilation that confront every man in politics. He had used his superabundant resources of mind, to fight wherever the prime abuse of power enlisted his will.

It was a good thing that he possessed a tough and disciplined will. This aging constitutionalist was no sleeper. He did not define man's happiness in terms of ease or rest—not even now that he had returned to Montpelier, showered by grateful citizens with offerings of mediocre but well-meant poetry and prose, and the small material gifts that even republican zealots deemed conscientiously permissible. His personal belief about the conduct of life he put into the simplest possible message, on greeting the members of the Princeton Whig Society in 1827, writing to them: "Receive and reflect the lights which will best prepare its members for a useful life, which alone can promise a happy one."[1] In his Virginia way, he was saying what the forthright Dr. Witherspoon had long ago often preached to the boys: "Do not live useless and die contemptible!"

Madison's first plan, so far as we can see it, was to use his remaining years in strictly private retirement. He would keep out of politics; read everything he could crowd into the day; enjoy the remarkably affectionate companionship of his agreeable wife; try to set his errant stepson, Payne Todd, straight; welcome his neighbors and friends; play with his nieces and nephews (there was a regular squadron of them); ride out daily and attend to his plantings; do something for the improvement of agriculture, perhaps organize a society; keep up his correspondence; and wait daily, *eagerly*, for the newspapers and the mail. Moreover, there were papers he wanted to put in order, events in those "great transactions" in which he had taken a part that he wanted to clarify for his countrymen. In any event, he was reported to have looked ineffably happy upon his release from the White House. He *might* have believed that private life would be all. To one part of his soul, there was the fair and modest dream of meditation; a Ulysses come home at last, choosing for the next round of life the lot of the simple shepherd. But to another part, there was his conscience, the will, fortified by habit, to find happiness by being useful. He would not live "useless," as it turned out.

Nothing serves to underline more sharply the heavy burdens Madison assumed to continue serving his country in his declining years than the last message, "Advice To My Country," which he deposited in his papers for posthumous publication. You may recall that Madison's "advice" was an urgent and solemn warning, closing with an entreaty:

> The advice nearest to my heart and deepest in my convictions is that the Union of the States be cherished and perpetuated. Let the open enemy to it be regarded as a Pandora with her box opened; and the disguised one, as the Serpent creeping with his deadly wiles into Paradise.[2]

So rarely does one find a hint of melodrama in Madison's controlled discourse that his message is doubly disturbing. Nor is the tone of prophetism congenial to his temper. For all his youthful study of the Scriptures and theology, Madison instinctively preferred the Golden Mean to the craggy extremes of prediction and revelation. Why, then, did he feel so deeply that the Union was in danger? Who was the open enemy, who disguised? And what sort of earthly "Paradise" did he consider America to be, now that men might lose it? Knowing the nature of the coming danger, what could the old statesman do *this time* to contain its calamitous course?

It should be borne in mind that Madison was alone on the scene, of the eminent men of his generation. He had ticked off the losses himself. He wrote Jared Sparks in 1831, five years after the death of his greatest friend, Jefferson:

"I happen . . . to be the sole survivor of those who were members of the Revolutionary Congress prior to the close of the war; as I had been for some years of the members of the Convention of 1776 which formed the first Constitution of Virginia."[3] He was the only man who could survey, from firsthand experience, the whole advancing movement from Independence to the creation of the federal republic, through the decisive first decade of its bitter trials, to its vast growth under Jefferson's Louisiana Purchase, through his own administrations that had brought the "second" war of independence from Great Britain to a surprisingly propitious conclusion for the United States, and through the dozen years that had intervened between his end of term and the heated controversies widespread through the country in the administration of Andrew Jackson.

2

Yet for a brief period after Madison's return to Montpelier, it had looked as though the joys of private life might really be his portion. Montpelier was but thirty miles from Jefferson's Monticello, and on the way there were Madison's neighbors, the Barbours, and William Cabell

Rives, the young man who would become an able United States senator, Minister to France, and ultimately would edit Madison's papers and write his biography. Visitors—diplomats, friends, and neighbors—were pouring in to visit Mrs. Madison and the former President at Montpelier. A memoir by a member of the family later recalled: "None ever left without regret! Situated on the route to the far famed Virginia Springs, strangers, enquiring for the novelties of the neighborhood, were told at Orange Court House that they were only five miles from ex-President Madison's. The punctilious northerner often hesitated about the propriety of 'intruding' but the cordial welcome they would receive . . . assured them of the pleasure it gave the inmates of that household to gratify the wishes of others."[4] On July 5, 1817, Dolley Madison wrote with pleasure to her niece that they had seated ninety persons at once at table, and it had been easier than to entertain twenty-five in Washington. The tables had been "fixed on the lawn under a thick arbor. The dinner was profuse and handsome and the company very orderly." She closed, saying "I wish you had just such a country home as this—as I truly believe it is the happiest and most independent life."[5]

The next year Madison delivered a stunning paper before The Agricultural Society of Albemarle, a high-spirited paper, full of comparisons of agricultural practice in his day with other cultures and civilizations, and evidencing an assured knowledge of the economics and sociology of agriculture. In a strange and utterly convincing way the reader of that paper, even today, can see a man in his element, turning easily to a subject that delighted him, and seeing it with imagination, in its widest bearings. In this context, we should not be surprised that Madison found he had something to say about the advantages of America. "In what other portion of . . . [the globe] will be found climates more friendly to the health or congenial to the feelings of its inhabitants? In what other, a soil yielding more food with not more labor? And above all, where will be found institutions equally securing the blessings of personal independence and social enjoyment? The enviable condition of the people of the United States, is often ascribed to the physical advantages of their soil and climate, and to their uncrowded situation. Much is certainly due to these causes —but a just estimate of the happiness of our country, will never overlook what belongs to the fertile activity of a free people, and the benign influence of a responsible government."[6]

These themes, the goodness of climate, soil, and other natural advantages the North American continent offered to industrious and artful men, and especially to the oppressed and poor of Europe, was an old one, proudly used by Madison from the days of the Revolution on. But Madison thrust aside almost casually the thesis that America's wildernesses, or her rich resources, her abundant virgin land, or even "the absence of a feudal past" (that darling maxim of modern political scientists), *determined* the role America would play. Madison assumed confidently that good sense would dictate a just estimate of the task of men here, as well as of the cooperating framework of natural resources. No one with good sense, he felt, could ever overlook "what belongs to the fertile activity of a free people, and the benign influence of a responsible government. . . ."

His own past, however, was against the perpetuation of a gentleman-farmer existence. Better still to say his own past was himself and he could not be cut off from urgent public concerns, when "the cause of liberty" was at stake.

3

In his retirement, Madison was fond of telling a little joke that went like this. In the public celebrations that took place in Philadelphia after the Convention had formed the Constitution, lawyers marched in the procession of trades and professions. They carried a banner, announcing that their motto was "truth." Among the spectators, there was a lady who voiced surprise. But when the wind blew the flag, she saw the reverse side, and exclaimed: "Ah! I see. It is 'truth,' on *both sides*."[7]

Embarrassments of this nature were faced by Madison in the closing decades of his life, when his authoritative knowledge of the constitutional system—which none could dispute or match—could nonetheless be scrutinized in its long course over the years and scored for inconsistencies. What Madison had written and said could also be confronted by episodes drawn from his career in public service, not only in Virginia and in the Federal Congress, but in his high offices as Secretary of State and as President. From Madison no one would have accepted a Whitmanesque dodge—"Do I contradict myself? Very well, I contradict myself."

—not from a statesman whose reputation as the prime master of political logic in the country was established.

A prominent instance of Madison's supposed "inconsistency" was the National Bank issue. Madison, having fought the first Bank of the United States as unconstitutional when Hamilton proposed it, changed it in its early years when he was the President. After the War of 1812, he took note of the financial chaos of the state banks and conceded the constitutional authority of Congress to enact such legislation. Accordingly, in April 1816, the Second United States Bank was created. One can imagine, therefore, a wry smile on Madison's face when later, in the midst of Jackson's war on the Bank, he received a letter from a young New Englander who wrote that the lyceum in Vermont was debating whether the Bank should be rechartered and remarked that Madison's opinion was being very strongly relied on, *on both sides* of the question.

The moral of these anecdotes is that Madison did appear to have taken both sides in significant questions about the meaning of the Constitution. This was charged of his position not only on the Bank, but on a considerable set of other issues, including a tariff to protect new

American industries, a system of roads and canals, and a strengthened military defense system. All these supposed turnabouts, the kind of charge that became the major design of the ironic exposé by Henry Adams of the Republicans in power "out-Federalizing the Federalists," do insistently raise the question what Madison meant when he fervently asserted that the Constitution was indeed "fundamental law." How, demand the critics, distinguish between the set of fundamental laws and a thing of wax that can be turned this way or that with a little pressure and, if need be, a little heat?

What is involved here is the perennial question about constitutions: what *do* they mean? In particular, since constitutions are framed to establish the basic institutions of government, and since those of a free society are framed to express the consent of the people to such institutions, what happens, as it must inevitably, when change of all sorts arises? At the initial level, this is a question of interpretation for those who swear to uphold the Constitution, whether the executive, the legislative, or those who work at deciding the constitutional issues on the cases that come before them as judges. In a broader setting, but still definable in relatively easy and practical terms, it involves the question of amendment, when new changes are of such a character that some of the existing institutions initially established by the Constitution can not be harmonized with the new conditions. But in the most philosophical sense, it involves the question of how to maintain a free society that is ordained by a constitution that initially sets it up recognizing that liberty cannot be caught in the fixed phrases of a given group of men, however great.

Madison, acute as always, knew exactly the nature of the game of interpretation. Continuing to the very end to comment on constitutional questions as they became, in turn, relevant to prominent problems of the time, he obviously continued to believe that he knew something essential about it that others might not see. About the *purely* theoretical puzzles he had not much concern. Men who did not have to brush with real politics could afford to speculate and dispute endlessly. "Theories," he said, "are the offspring of the closet; exceptions to them, the lessons of experience." [8] He himself was prepared by lifelong training to inhabit the midworld of theories tested in experience, and modified to solve the most urgent problems ahead. He was profoundly impressed with the lessons of experience in one sense; that only those who knew the history of the Revolutionary period, and the "gloomy chaos" which preceded the Constitution, could properly evaluate the multiple good that had resulted from its order. Of course, he also understood that he might be accused of a protective fondness for the Constitution he had done so much to bring about. Granting that in the interpretations of the Constitution he was influenced by his knowledge of the men and points of view of the time, he suggested with ironic understatement that men who interpreted it "without a danger of that bias" were more likely to misinterpret than was he. The greatest difficulty of all in interpreting the Constitution at a period removed in time from the original context was a semantic difficulty —what Madison called the problem of "the silent innovations of time on the meaning of words and phrasing." For this he knew no corrective except resorting to the record, to the Debates in the Federal Convention, and to the Ratifying Conventions and other documents of the time to achieve an understanding of the history, which might properly open the meaning of its text.

In dealing with this question of the meaning of the Constitution, and Madison's inconsistent turnabouts, we should discriminate two classes of cases. The first class arises from the exercise of powers which rest on implicit rather than explicit powers. These include the issues of internal improvements, the tariff, the National Bank, etc. In this class Madison originally opposed the measures when they were advanced by Hamilton in the first stages of the Federal Government, on the grounds that the Constitution did not enumerate these powers. But his real fear was twofold: one, that an extension of powers so early in the history of the Republic would establish dangerous precedents with no limits and undermine the constitutional enterprise of limiting federal government. But his second fear was even more substantial. Whether correctly or not, he judged that Hamilton had little concern for popular sovereignty on which the compact was based, and that he had primary concern for energetic government, for a strong union to support special interests that he favored (for personal or policy reasons) and for his own power. I must confess that I believe there was ample warrant for these fears and that part of this was brilliantly established in Mr. Boyd's "Number 7."[9] In this connection, the realistic Madison was containing the so-called "realistic" Hamilton. Therefore, when the Republicans came into power and no longer needed to fear the unprincipled use of the Constitution for ends of a national but undemocratic sort, it was possible to accept certain items from the Federalist program which would promote the common interest. However, I do not intend to examine the constitutional issues raised by this class of cases.

The second class of cases bears directly and profoundly on the whole issue of the Union established by the Constitution. These cases have to do with the matter of states' rights, and whether the states can dissolve the Union. There are two periods which are critical in our history and in which Madison was moved to probe the meaning of the Constitution. The first period relates to the crisis stemming from the Alien and Sedition Acts in the 1790's. The second period relates to the ominous sectional conflicts of the 1830's. In each of these cases Madison was reviewing states' rights in relation to the power of the federal government. In the first case he appears to oppose the Union on behalf of states' rights. In the second case he appears to uphold the Union against the claims of states' rights. In taking these two apparently contradictory positions, he seems indeed to take both sides. Since the second class of cases goes right to the core of his theory of a federal republic as a just society, it is imperative that we understand his position and see that he remained constant in his attachment to "the cause of liberty."

4

I will not rehearse the facts of the Alien and Sedition Acts, nor the details of the Kentucky and Virginia Resolutions which protested those laws as oppressive and reactionary violations of guaranteed constitutional freedoms. Elsewhere, I have tried to show that while there were differences between Jefferson and Madison on how far to carry these protests, they were both turning to the people in the states as bulwarks guarding "persecuted man" from losing his political freedom through the inroads on free speech, free press, and a policy of easy naturalization for immigrants who wished to become citizens. All these values were hurt by the illiberal laws.[10] Both Jefferson and Madison knew well that under these laws the Federalists would close down Republican newspapers, arrest editors and publishers, and cripple or smash the vital line of news and political intelligence that alone could keep the opposition party going as a significant party capable of turning the Federalists out of office. Under such total provocation, Jefferson unwisely talked of the right of a state to declare a federal law "null, void, and of no force or effect." At Madison's insistence, these words were stricken out of the Virginia Resolution, and his preferred language restored. That language merely urged the other states to concur with Virginia "in declaring, as it does hereby declare, that the acts aforesaid are unconstitutional." He thus put himself on sure ground, refraining from assuming that the state legislature could claim for itself judicial functions, and advocating only a justifiable expression of opinion from the states.

When the New England states replied indignantly to the invitations from Virginia and Kentucky to join in protesting the usurpation of rights by the Federal Government, some of them reaffirming their support of the Alien and Sedition Acts, Madison was requested to prepare a report, reviewing the grounds for the earlier protests. This is his lengthy *Report of 1800,* which deserves to be far better known than it is.[11] Always at his best in a careful and orderly examination of fundamentals, Madison provides in this *Report* his first searching review of the American constitutional system since the era, a decade earlier, when he wrote his Federalist papers and debated in the Virginia Ratifying

Convention. I need not re-create the texture of confluent argument in this *Report,* but will merely indicate the major points of Madison's position.

The most fundamental point concerned the essence of a free government. He wrote: "The right of electing the members of the Government constitutes . . . the essence of a free and responsible government. The value and efficacy of this right depends on the knowledge of the comparative merits and demerits of the candidates for public trust, and on the equal freedom, consequently, of examining and discussing these merits and demerits of the candidates respectively."[12] No free government can exist under the provisions of the Sedition Act is the message of his *Report.* Opposition political parties—the minimum of at least two parties that are putatively candidates for power—are essential to prevent a state from becoming a total state. But if, in the language of the Sedition Act, persons who conspired to oppose measures of the government, or who promoted riots or unlawful assemblies, or who published "*any false, scandalous, and malicious writings*" (italics added) against the government or its officials could be fined and punished by imprisonment—then clearly the situation of the competitors to the party in power was *not equal:* because, said Madison in his mild language, "the characters of the former will be covered by the Sedition Act from animadversion exposing them to disrepute among the people, whilst that latter may be exposed to the contempt and hatred of the people, without a violation of the act." This disables more than the competitors, more than the "outs" who would like to have an equal chance to get "*in.*" "What will be the situation of the people," Madison asked, if such an act stands. "Not free; because they will be compelled to make their election between competitors whose pretensions they are not permitted by the act equally to examine, to discuss, and to ascertain. And from both these situations will not those in power derive an undue advantage for continuing themselves in it, which, by impairing the right of election, endangers the blessings of the Government founded on it?" This line of thought upholds the "justice" of what the Virginia Resolutions were protesting; for "the right of freely examining public characters and measures, and of free communication thereone, is the only effectual guardian of every other right," Madison concludes.[13]

That the Constitution protected this essential

right of free communication and political criticism he thought indisputable on the basis of the First Amendment, as it was even earlier explicitly protected by the act of ratification by the Virginia Ratifying Convention that approved the Constitution. He then developed the notion that if there was no violation or impropriety in declaring the Alien and Sedition Acts to be unconstitutional within one state, there was "no trace of improper means" in communicating the declaration to other "sister" states. In fact, were the states to express their disapproval and alarm at these laws invading the freedom of the human mind and poisoning the wells of political choice, they would be forgetting one of the strongest arguments used in the establishment of the General Government. Here Madison recalled that those who apprehended danger to liberty from a government entrusted with ruling so large a country, had, during the debates on ratification, listened receptively to the appeal that there would be intermediate state governments "between the people and that Government," whose "vigilance . . . [to] descry the first symptoms of usurpation; and . . . sound the alarm to the public" would preclude significant danger to liberty.[14]

All these things being so, Madison then pointed out that the concluding resolutions of Virginia had noticed that "warm affection to the Union and its members . . . that scrupulous fidelity to the Constitution, which have been invariably felt by the people of this State." He drove home this point, saying that the part which Virginia had borne in the "establishing of our National Independence, in the establishment of our National Constitution, and in maintaining under it the authority and laws of the Union" should suffice to expose the falseness of any insinuation attacking her "national patriotism." On the contrary, the Virginia Resolutions themselves provide "the strongest evidence of attachment both to the Constitution and to the Union, since it is only by maintaining the different governments and departments within their respective limits that the blessings of either can be perpetuated." The *Report* closed with a resolution stating the adherence of the state to the Resolutions of 1798 as "founded in truth, as consonant with the Constitution, and as conducive to its preservation." And it unhesitatingly renewed its protest against the Alien and Sedition Acts as "palpable and alarming infractions of the Constitution." [15]

5

This provides the essential background for the contribution Madison made, in his role as constitutional commentator, in the nineteen years of his valuable retirement. He was still eager to maintain some sort of equilibrium between the general and the state governments as the pivot on which the federal system turned. Indeed, this was at once the unique virtue and the Gordian knot of the American system. As he suggested to Spencer Roane in 1821, it would be most desirable if the concurrent track on which the states and the general government exercised separate jurisdictions could develop into a system of mutual cooperation, rather than one of mutual checks and hindrances. This suggestion, incidentally, is of great interest at this very moment in our history when the role of the state governments in administering welfare and education programs and other related programs for rebuilding the cities, is once again being reviewed and upgraded. As Madison was coming to see it in the 1820's, the states possessed a variety of means to combat usurpations threatened from the federal government. Most importantly, they might change that government through election or amendment—or even, if need be, through impeachment. They might indeed change it also through revolution—but that he put to one side for separate consideration and judgment. On the other hand, the federal government could resort to judicial review as its great defense against encroachments by the states upon its proper authorities.

The great issue of the era, however, was the one which struck at the continuance of the whole constitutional, federal system: the issue of nullification. Everything points to the understandable fact that Madison would dearly have loved to keep himself out of the battle—he knew at once that this was the most dangerous issue afloat, and that it might end by disrupting the Union and covering with war the once blessed inhabitants of the United States. It was an issue on which he was particularly loath to speak out, since he knew that there was ground for sectional quarrel and he believed that in one sense the equal liberty of the Southern states had *not* been given just economic treatment compared with the interests of the North. His attachments, his friendships, his loyalty to place and region were very real. And much would depend on his stated views—as a realist, he knew that, too.

When the Webster-Hayne debate stood sharp

in the center of the nation's troubled gaze, both Webster and Hayne sought Madison's support. That was the opening of the new decade, 1830, and Madison declined open comment, even though the contest turned on opposed constitutional doctrines. Hayne, speaking for South Carolina, maintained that the states were sovereign; that as sovereign parties to the compact that created the Constitution, they retained the right of full and complete interposition if rights were infringed, and that that certainly included the right of nullification. Webster, speaking for Massachusetts, rebutted the historical account of the Constitution his opponent had offered, stating that the states are sovereign only so far as their power was not qualified by the Constitution, and that the Constitution and the national government are sovereign over the people. He denied that the Constitution was the result of a compact; it was meant to be a popular government, of distributed powers. That distribution of powers was meant to be binding upon the national government and the states.

Although Madison declined to uphold the hand of either of the men, he did begin to filter his views through Nicholas P. Trist who was then in Washington, engaged in writing pamphlets denying a connection between Madison's Virginia Resolutions and the nullification movement. Trist had written Madison early in 1830 asking for suggestions, so the way was clear. Around that time he would refer correspondents who queried him on his views of nullification to Trist's essay on "Nullification Theory." In the spring of 1830, however, when he received a copy of Senator Hayne's speeches which the Senator had sent him, Madison composed a letter that was itself an unambiguous repudiation of Hayne's position and a definition of his own—virtually an essay, of over 2,500 words.[16]

The letter moved like a mowing machine over the field of Hayne's arguments. The character of the Constitution of the United States was not that of a compact between the states and the General Government. "The idea of a compact between the Governors & the Governed was exploded with the Royal doctrine that Government was held by some tenure independent of the people." It was not formed by the states as individual government, but by the people of each State, acting in their highest sovereign capacity through Conventions (as with State Constitutions). The Constitution was therefore a compact between the states only in this sense; and in this sense the people in their sovereign capacity decided to grant authority to the general government over one people for specified objects. That authority of the general government cannot be revoked or changed at the will of any state. Thus, the government of the United States created by the Constitution is government "in as strict a sense of the term" as those of the states. Besides, Madison pursued, it was foreseen that provision must be made for deciding controversies concerning the boundary of jurisdiction, otherwise conflicts of physical force might ensue. "A political system that does not provide for a peaceable & authoritative termination of . . . controversies, can be but the bane & shadow of a Government; the very object & end of a real Government being the substitution of law & order for uncertainty confusion & violence." [17] Such final decision of controversies could not be left to thirteen discordant states—or to twenty-four "with a prospective increase"! Disorganization and even decomposition of the Union would follow upon such an imbecility. A uniform authority of the laws is in itself a vital principle, he explained. That is why the Constitution provided that "This Constitution, and the Laws which shall be made in Pursuance therof; and all Treaties made, or which shall be made, under the Authority of the United States, shall be the supreme Law of the Land."

His examination had disclosed that "any reference to constitutional right in an individual State to arrest by force the operation of a law of the United States" is wholly unwarranted. He pointed to his *Report of 1800* for confirmation of this truth, and noted especially that Virginia's protest dealt with a statement of *opinion and sentiments* and the attempt to achieve "*concert,*" i.e., *agreement,* from the other states in like declarations. "The term *nullification* to which such an important meaning is now attached, was never a part of the Resolutions and appears not to have been contained in the Kentucky Resolutions as originally passed, but to have been introduced at an after date," [18] wrote Madison. He was strictly correct in this statement; and it is still not known who drafted the *second* set of Kentucky Resolutions where the word "nullification" does appear. Madison did not reveal this (nor indeed was he bound to), that Jefferson had words to that effect in his original first draft for Kentucky, but that these had been deleted before the Kentucky Legislature acted upon them. Later, when he refreshed his memory by looking at the manuscripts, he admitted this to Edward Everett,[19] but he commented: "Still

I believe that he did not attach to it [nullification] the idea of a constitutional right in the sense of S. Carolina, but that of a natural one in cases justly appealing to it."

Now he was ready to move to the most serious question of all, having clearly ruled that nullification was not allowable as a prerogative of a single state, nor even as the prerogative of a group of states within the constitutional union. What of the extreme case, however, where a state, having resorted to all its constitutional means to protest abuses of power, witnesses their accumulation; weighs passive obedience and nonresistance against resistance and revolution; and decides that nonresistance is the greater evil? There is then only one resort, the last of all, "the appeal . . . to natural rights and the law of self-preservation." But this, said Madison, is "the Ultima ratio, under all Governments, whether consolidated, confederated, or partaking of both those characters." In such an extremity, he distinctly stated, a state would have "a right, tho it would be a natural not a *constitutional* Right to make the appeal" (italics added). And the same might be said of particular portions of any political community whatsoever "so expressed as to be driven to a choice between the alternative evils." [20]

In innumerable letters and papers he wrote later on the subject, he exposed the absurdity of South Carolina imagining that it was in this extremity and "so oppressed." And yet South Carolina wanted to nullify on the ground of its *constitutional* right. Madison's answer to Hayne was never made public by the latter, for obvious reasons. But Madison himself in the matter of a few months incorporated much of the argument in an even more exhaustive letter to Edward Everett, which he knew Everett would print in the *North American Review*. Madison had thus, in the summer of 1830, publicly washed his hands of the "nullifying doctrine." To many Southerners, he was henceforth "The Enemy Within!"

6

Just as his early years had been devoted to "the cause of liberty," his last years were wholly absorbed in defending the Union. Calhoun and his followers felt the reproof administered to them by the old sage at Montpelier, when he entered into friendly correspondence with Thomas Smith Grimké, the leader of the South Carolina Union cause and the most eminent lawyer of the Charleston bar, who learned the logic of his arguments from a close study of Madison's position. But we have looked at Madison's overt position thus far, and have not paused to ask what the Union meant to him that he would vest his remaining years in its cause.

It seems that even though Madison had become conspicuous as a foe of nullification, the states' rights leaders and publicists would not give up their claims upon him. Surely, they wrote, he believed in the right of the states to secede peaceably from the Union! Madison was aghast. He had already come to see the Union as "the last hope of mankind." He had written to Lafayette, for instance, urging a federal system for France, saying it was an absolute necessity for any large republic.[21] And he had written a memo on the federal principle, indicating that it could be extended almost indefinitely through a "pyramid of Federal systems," the germ of a thought of world federalism that he occasionally permitted himself to contemplate, despite his habit of throwing cold water on utopian projects.[22] He was filled with apprehension at the thought that nullification and secession sentiment might shatter the union which had brought such indisputable blessings of freedom and advancing welfare to the American people, warning if the Federal Union were dissolved it would be impossible ever to renew it, as was "brought home to every mind by the difficulties encountered in establishing it." By thus recalling the heroic labors, the "*almost-not*" creation of the Federal Union, he was pleading for his countrymen to envisage the consequences of jumping from the frying pan into the fire. Would jealousies among the various new nations that would exist if the Union were sundered, be less? or more? To flee the United States government because of its so-called "consolidation" might teach the heaviest of all lessons to the seceding states—they would soon find themselves in governments "of a more consolidating and monarchical tendency than the greatest jealousy has charted on the existing system." [23]

All very well, but what did Madison see in the Union to call out his highest loyalty? The answer is the hope, and the chance "for a common lasting improvement" in the lot of man. The spirit of compromise that had fed into the American Experiment, he firmly believed was capable of encouraging more human opportunity than other systems, even mild ones like the society English liberals were trying to bring about but that still was redolent of "too much nobility . . . to flatter the popular hopes, and too much of the spirit of the Caste . . . to meet that of the nation, on any ground on which Reform can be stationary."[24]

But if the Union meant a new kind of society, a free and just society, ever advancing, how can we square this ideal with the actuality of slavery? It is essential that we face this question, particularly today.

Perhaps the best introduction to this matter is provided by some perceptive observation made by Harriet Martineau after she had visited Madison in 1834. This brilliant English political economist and reformer commented that Madison was "a wonderful man of eighty-three. His voice was clear and strong, and his manner of speaking particularly lively, often playful!" She wrote that "His finest characteristic was his inexhaustible faith that a well-founded commonwealth would be made immortal by the spirit of justice its principles instilled in the people." This belief she found shone brightly in Madison's talk—except on one topic. "With regard to slavery he owned himself almost to be in despair . . . acknowledging . . . all the evils with which it has ever been charged . . . . He observed that the whole Bible is against negro slavery; but that the clergy do not preach this, and the people do not see it."[25]

The despair which Miss Martineau observed

is, I believe, directly connected with the urgent message of "Advice To My Country" which Madison decided to write. Indeed, his decisive repudiation of the Southern pro-slavery extremists, which doubtless was required by many of his basic values and principles, could also find sufficient explanation in his strong convictions about the evil of slavery and his absolute refusal to lend himself to a movement that would in any way justify the peculiar institution as good. Let me indicate briefly just what Madison's views on slavery were.

7

From his early youth, Madison believed that the institution of slavery was unquestionably a great moral evil, and while still undecided on his permanent career, wrote to Edmund Randolph that he wished to provide a decent and independent subsistence for himself, "to depend as little as possible on the labour of slaves." [26] His concern over slavery throughout his life was similar to Jefferson's, Washington's, George Wythe's, George Mason's, Edmund Randolph's, and other conscientious and humanitarian Virginians.[27] A letter to his father, when Madison was in Philadelphia in 1783, discussed the problem of a Madison slave, "Billey," whom he would not force back to Virginia "even if [it] could be done; and have accordingly taken measures for his final separation from me." Madison added that he could not think of punishing him by transportation "merely for coveting that liberty for which we have paid the price of so much blood, and have proclaimed so often to be the right, and worthy the pursuit, of every human being." [28] This statement to his father is one of many ways in which Madison manifested his troubled conscience about the intolerable hypocrisy of slavery in a country that had declared its independence in terms of equality, life, liberty, and the pursuit of happiness.

In the Constitutional Convention, Madison entered the debate over the slave trade clause, protesting that he "thought it wrong to admit in the Constitution the idea that there could be property in men" [29] and he explained in the Virginia Convention that he accepted the "1808 clause" (instead of immediate prohibition of the slave trade) because the compromise was necessary to secure the support of the Deep South states, South Carolina and Georgia. In the *Federalist* papers, Madison had made similar points without, of course, mentioning the difficult states by name. In Number 38 he conceded several defects in the Constitution, which he nonetheless thought far overbalanced by the good it promised—as indicated in his question "Is the importation of slaves permitted by the new Constitution for twenty years. By the old it is permitted forever." [30] The measure of his hope on this issue may be seen in Number 42, where he wrote: "It ought to be considered as a great point gained in favor of humanity, that a period of twenty years may terminate forever, within these States, a traffic which has so long and so loudly upbraided the barbarism of modern policy; that within that period, it will receive a considerable discouragement from the Federal government . . . ." [31]

His view was not only that slavery was a crime against humanity, but that it was the source of the slothful corruption of free white men in laboring for themselves and a grave danger to the peace and security of the Union. He did not merely say so and write so, but acted as and when he could. In addition to the positions he took in the Constitutional Convention and the First Congress, when Madison became President he vigorously pursued Jefferson's earlier attempt to stamp out the slave trade by effective national laws. Jefferson, in 1806, asked Congress to do everything possible to be ready with an effective law prohibiting the slave trade so that when the day stipulated in the Constitution arrived (Jan. 1, 1808) it could instantly be put into effect. Jefferson seized the occasion to put the full force of his moral condemnation of the slave trade before the public. He called for action to withdraw the citizens of the United States "from all further participation in those violations of human rights which have been so long continued on the unoffending inhabitants of Africa, and which the morality, the reputation, and the best interests of our country, have long been eager to proscribe."[32] Congress complied, enacted a law prohibiting the slave trade and providing forfeitures and fines upon ships and crews engaged in the slave traffic.

Nonetheless, it was necessary for Madison to take up the challenge in his administration, and he was determined to suppress the "evil" trade. In 1810, he pointed out to Congress that abuses still were being committed under the American flag: "it appears that American citizens are instrumental in carrying on the traffic in enslaved Africans, equally in violation of the laws of humanity and the defiance of those of their own country." He urged Congress to devise "further" means to bring about the entire suppression of the trade.[33] After the War of 1812,

Madison again requested Congress in his Annual Message of 1816 to use its legislative power to the full in punishing violators. He gave urgency to his request by setting American practices alongside those of other European nations.

> The United States, having been the first to abolish within the extent of their authority the transportation of the natives of Africa into slavery, by prohibiting the introduction of slaves and by punishing their citizens participating in the traffic, can not but be gratified at the progress made by concurrent efforts of other nations toward a general suppression of so great an evil. They must feel at the same time the greater solicitude to give the fullest efficacy to their own regulations. With that view, the interposition of Congress appears to be required by the violations and evasions which . . . are chargeable on unworthy citizens who mingle in the slave trade under foreign flags and with foreign ports, and by collusive importations of slaves into the United States through adjoining ports and territories. I present the subject to Congress with a full assurance of their disposition to apply all the remedy which can be afforded by an amendment of the law. The regulations

> which were intended to guard against abuses of a kindred character in the trade between several States ought also to be rendered more effectual for their humane object.[34]

For those who are tone-deaf to deep sentiment when it is voiced in a public message or address, there is something to ponder in Madison's *unpublicized* conduct while he was President. Mr. Brant's biography of Madison calls attention to the fact that he did more than castigate the slave trade on public occasions. In 1810, Madison sent a copy of a dispatch which he seems to have written himself to the American Minister in Great Britain, William Pinkney. He sent Dr. Benjamin Rush a confidential copy knowing his anti-slavery views. The dispatch endorsed Great Britain's action condemning an American slave ship and rejecting the owners' indignant complaint that the Negroes were slaves under American law. The dispatch pointed out that since these men had been brought forcibly from their own country, might they not be "treated as prisoners of war liberated by their entrance within a neutral jurisdiction?" It also suggested that another tack might be taken: these men were not part of the crew and thus might "be viewed in the light of passengers held in false imprisonment."[35] Many years earlier Madison had protested that human beings should not be viewed as property. He welcomed the chance to do what he could, within the limitations of the powers of his office and the social and constitutional realities that were binding upon a public official.

In the period of Madison's retirement, he pondered and discussed the methods of getting rid of the peculiar institution entirely. He knew how tragically complicated the problem of slavery was. His analysis of the situation usually represented a blend of idealistic reform with realistic descriptions of what he called "existing and probably unalterable prejudices" on the part of the great mass of the American people. He believed that the difference between the black and the white races were permanent, although nothing he said or wrote stated that they were naturally inferior. Amalgamation of the two races, he thought, was unacceptable even as an ideal, while a perfect equality on social, political, and economic terms he thought unattainable in fact. The latter consideration made him favor a method of gradual emancipation through colonization, since he thought that if the freed Negroes remained among the whites "under the degrading privations of equal rights, political or social, they must be always dissatisfied with their condition as a change only from one to another species of oppression."[36] He became a life member of the American Colonization Society, upon its formation in 1813, and subsequently he accepted the Vice-Presidency of the Virginia branch of the Society. In 1834, he regretted that he was too old and feeble to accept the Presidency of the American Colonization Society to which he had been unanimously elected.[37] The year before, he had argued in a detailed letter against the learned defense of slavery and concomitant attack on the American Colonization Society written by Thomas Dew, professor of history, metaphysics, and political law in William and Mary College. Dew's pamphlet, *Review of the Debate in the Virginia Legislature of 1831 and 1832*, has been regarded as perhaps the most effective defense ever made of slavery; it soon became *the* political classic for pro-slavery advocates. Madison's polite but flinty critique of Dew's position defended the policy of emancipation via colonization, examined and then dismissed Dew's arithmetical calculations destined to show that colonization was impracticable because "requiring an expense and sacrifice of property far beyond the resources of the States and Federal

Governments," and pointedly stated that the essential considerations were not the expense, but (1) the "attainment of the requisite Asylums" (of favorable economic potential for the colonists); (2) the consent of the individuals to be removed; and (3) the labor to fill the vacuum to be created.[38]

Madison's willingness to sustain the activities of the Colonization Society, which was financed entirely by voluntary contributions, led him to think seriously about the financing of a long-range emancipation program. As he defined the goal of colonization, it was to extinguish slavery. In 1832, the Colonization Society of Virginia had John Marshall as president, and Madison, vice-president. They requested the legislature to provide public money to aid the colony in Liberia. Madison also thought that the Federal government could be drawn upon to support an extensive program from its sale of western lands.[39]

8

But nothing is more fascinating than a personal relationship that throws much light on Madison's views and indeed on the ultimate judgment that we may be led to make about them.

I cannot tell this story in anything like the detail it deserves—only its most salient points.

Edward Coles was Madison's personal secretary for six years during the latter's Presidency. He was the son of a well-to-do planter family in Albemarle County, well educated, intelligent, personable. Coles was related to Dolley Madison and became an intimate member of the Presidential family in Washington.

He was intensely idealistic and while still a student at William and Mary College "became convinced that man could not rightfully have a property in his fellow man; and not being able to reconcile slavery as it existed in Virginia, with my feelings and principles, I determined to free my slaves and leave the State." [40] Apparently he wanted to do this as soon as he inherited his share of the family estate, including some twenty slaves, when his father died in 1808, but enormous obstacles had to be overcome. Virginia laws would make the emancipation meaningless, and he had to seek some place where his slaves, once restored to freedom, could become self-supporting, educated, and fully responsible moral beings.[41] He actually accepted the post as secretary to Madison in order to avail himself of opportunities in Washington to find out more about what part of the nonslaveholding section of the country it would be best to settle in.

It was not until 1818 that he was finally to put his long-cherished plan into effect. He gathered his slaves together for a long journey, took horses, cattle, and farm implements and started the most unusual trek to Illinois that history, which *is* stranger than fiction, records. They rode to Brownsville and there Coles purchased three flatboats. The entire party descended the Ohio to New Albany. Just as they were in sight, Coles, who had not yet divulged his intention to his slaves, called them together on deck to tell them the glad tidings. His account of this experience is too interesting to parphrase.[42]

> Being curious to see the effect of an instantaneous severing of the manacles of bondage, and letting loose on the buoyant wings of liberty the long pent up spirit of man, I . . . made them a short address . . . and concluded my remarks by so expressing myself, that by a turn of a sentence, I proclaimed in the shortest and fullest manner possible, they were no longer slaves, but free—free as I was, and were at liberty to proceed with me, or to go ashore at their pleasure.

The effect on them was electrical. They stared at me and at each other, as if doubting the accuracy or reality of what they heard. In breathless silence they stood before me, unable to utter a word, but with countenances beaming with expression which no words could convey, and which no language can now describe. As they began to see the truth of what they had heard, and to realize their situation, there came on a kind of hysterical, giggling laugh. After a pause of intense and unutterable emotion, bathed in tears, and with tremulous voices, they gave vent to their gratitude, and implored the blessings of God on me. When they had recovered, Ralph [one of Cole's slaves] said he thought I ought not to do it till they had repaid me the expenses I had been at in removing them from Virginia, and had improved my farm and "gotten me well fixed in that new country." To this, all simultaneously expressed their concurrence, and their desire to remain with me, as my servants, until they had comfortably fixed me at my new home.

I told them no. I had made up my mind to give to them immediate and unconditional freedom; that I had . . . been prevented by

> the delays, first in selling my property in Virginia, and then in collecting the money . . . That . . . as a reward for their past services, as well as a stimulant to their future exertions, and with a hope it would add to their self esteem and their standing in the estimation of others, I should give to each head of a family a quarter section, containing 160 acres of land. To this all objected, saying I had done enough for them in giving them their freedom. . . . I told them I had thought much of my duty and of their rights, and that it was due alike to both that I should do what I had said I should do; and accordingly, soon after reaching Edwardsville, I executed and delivered to them deeds to the lands promised them.

Coles' fate in Illinois may truly be called a splendid misery. He was hounded by pro-slavery groups, vilified, slapped with law suits on the charge that he had not given security for the good behavior of the slaves he was freeing, and fined—but managed to fight the case successfully in the courts. His charity and the uncharitable behavior of others towards him combined to almost ruin his finances. But he managed to be appointed register of the land office at Edwardsville; in 1822, after a bitter fight, he was elected Governor. The fight was over slavery in Illinois, for though it was nominally free territory, slavery existed there, and an ugly movement was growing to extend the institution and give it legal status by a specially convened Assembly. The outcome is that Governor Coles was able to play a leading role in the struggle over slavery in Illinois. In the centennial ceremonies for the states, Governor Frank Lowden wrote about Coles:

> It is almost certain that if it had not been for his persistence and courage, slavery would have been written into the Illinois Constitution. The story of his struggle against the forces of slavery is one of the most inspiring in the annals of Illinois. If he had failed . . . it is not likely that the great debate between Lincoln and Douglas would have occurred. It was this debate which made Lincoln President of the United States. Indeed, with Illinois a slave state, it is altogether possible that the Confederacy might have won. And thus the battle which Edward Coles, in the new and sparsely settled state, waged against the forces of slavery, becomes an event of historical importance of the first class.[43]

This young man continued always to occupy a special place in the affection of the Madisons. He was a great favorite with Mrs. Madison, who had occupied herself with the irresistible pastime of finding suitable candidates for him to marry (and failed; he chose his own), and Madison seemed to nourish for him an affection truly fatherly. One can imagine that six years of daily life together permitted many talks about the sin of slavery and methods of approaching a solution of the problem. For the subject was not only uppermost in Coles' mind and a continuing deep concern of Madison's, but Dolley Madison had earlier in life been a strict Quaker, loyal daughter of her conscientious parents. Her father, John Payne, was one of the first of the Society of Friends in Virginia to become convinced that slavery was a sin. He was called "a fanatic" for persisting in his belief even to the point of selling his plantation and freeing all his slaves. Payne moved to Philadelphia with his family in 1786, and with several of his devoted former slaves who refused to leave the family.[44] Dolley Madison's brother, John C. Payne (who became Madison's closest friend in the statesman's last years) continued the Payne family tradition by freeing his slaves.

After Coles had withdrawn from Virginia,

on principle, and had become Governor-elect of Illinois, Madison sent him a pedometer, with a humorous little note: "As you are about to assume new motives to walk in a straight path," he wrote, "and with measured steps, I wish you to accept the little article enclosed, as a type of the course I am sure you will pursue, & as a token of the affection I have so long cherished for you." [45] Madison even paid him the unmistakable compliment of a fatherly relationship; he minced no words when Coles made a mistake! Madison thought Coles had done so when he wrote in 1834, trying to get Madison to issue a blast at President Jackson and the Jacksonians on the issue of dictatorial power. Madison refused, plainly telling Coles he was wrong in thinking that nullification as a threat was on the decline "and less dangerous than the popularity of the President . . . what more dangerous than nullification, or more evident than the progress it continues to make, either in its original shape or in the disguises it assumes. Nullification has the effect of putting powder under the Constitution & Union, and a match in the hand of every party, to blow them up at pleasure." [46] On one issue Coles had needed no instruction. In many political matters, Madison always remained, easily, the master.

9

My purpose in introducing the Madison–Coles relationship in a discussion of Madison's beliefs on slavery is perhaps rising out of the mists by now. It is not at all to imply that Madison should be granted credit for Coles' determined abolitionism. *That,* the whole of the personal sacrifices, and the glory, were his and his alone. But it is important to recognize that Coles became dedicated to the cause of emancipation not as many of the later abolitionists did, on religious grounds, but explicitly on the heritage, which he valued so much, of the American Enlightenment—of the Declaration of Independence, of the American Experiment in free government. In 1814, Coles had written to Jefferson, urging the seventy-one-year-old statesman to throw his energies into leading the campaign for "a general emancipation of the slaves in Virginia," urging him to use the love and confidence society extended to him "to put into complete practice those hallowed principles contained in that renowned Declaration, of which you were the immortal author, and on which we founded our right to resist oppression and establish our freedom and independence." [47]

Jefferson replied as I believe Madison would reply. He agreed with whole heart in the object of the cause of emancipation; he adverted to the public concerns which had managed to absorb his time quite pressingly enough until his old age. Then he wrote:

> I had always hoped that the younger generation, receiving their early impressions after the flame of liberty had been kindled . . . and become . . . the vital spirit of every American . . . would have sympathized with *oppression wherever found*, and proved their love of liberty *beyond their own share of it.* (italics added)

Instead he had found apathy, and forgetfulness, even that others had fought earlier to win liberty for them! Yet, said Jefferson, "the hour of emancipation is advancing in the march of time. It will come. . . ." He then candidly expressed his own view about the means he thought preferable to the one Coles considered necessary—expatriating himself from his native state. Come forward in the public councils, "insinuate and inculcate it softly but steadily thro' the medium of writing and conversation, associate others in your labors, and when the phalanx is formed, bring on and press the proposition perseveringly until its accomplishment. . . . No good measure was ever proposed, which, if duly pursued, failed to prevail in the end. . . ." [48]

Ah yes, "in the end," the abolitionists would murmur, and we today murmur. "In the end," to paraphrase Keynes, "we will all be dead." But Jefferson and Madison knew the tragic depth and measure of the problem of the South's peculiar institution, and foresaw the avalanche of blood which irrational or overly hasty action might set flowing. They knew unless emancipation came gradually and with the consent not only of a section but of all the sections whose interests were deeply concerned, the legacy of prejudice and hatred would perpetuate itself for generations. I must admit that on any view, modern or old-fashioned, they should at least be granted reasonable grounds for vesting their hopes in colonization—even though, from a later perspective that appears to be patently an impractical and half hearted approach.

What we cannot fail to note about Madison, however, is the vastly practical aid he rendered to the advancing cause of liberty: that men some day, by other hands, *could* be set free if the Union were preserved. For this is what the Union meant for him: it was the earthly Paradise where all who valued it and kept its commands might walk free. *Fear two enemies*, he had said: the *open enemy*, who will plunder freedom, and *the disguised*—the zealots and the hypocrites who will mouth the maxims of freedom while they goad free men on, to break the commands of Paradise—and plunge downward into Paradise *Lost!*

10

In these pages I have tried to engage your thought on only three strands of Madison's inventive genius and his steadfast heart. He had chosen *liberty*, while young and impressionable; he had pursued it in his middle years by searching for a new form of *justice;* he had protected both in his old age, in his grand effort to weld the South to the Union in the hope that the larger interest would remove injustice to men on account of race.

He could not have all he desired, even when the desires were for others, and good. But surely, above all, *he* understood that. Charles Jared Ingersoll visited Madison a month before he died and found him clearly aware of his condition; "Infirm as his body is, his understanding is as bright as ever; his intelligence, recollections, discriminations, and philosophy, all delightfully instructive.[49] His faithful brother-in-law, John C. Payne, reported to a friend in June 1836: "In his views on important subjects, the same soundness, clearness, vigor and felicity of expression now prevail that have ever distinguished his compositions; and the same richness and playfulness of imagination, the same draughts from the stores of memory." [50] George Tucker, who had consulted Madison closely as he prepared a two-volume biography of Thomas Jefferson, at last sent the galleys to his mentor and in mid-June a copy arrived, bearing the dedication of the volumes to James Madison. Consequently on June 27, the day before his life came to a close, Madison made a great effort to dictate a significant acknowledgement to Tucker, and somehow managed to write his own signature.[51] Everyone in touch with Madison, and each of his late visitors at Montpelier, had noted his serene and active spirit despite his infirmities. Paul Jennings' eyewitness account of Madison's last words fulfill these observations. Jennings said that breakfast was brought up, as usual.

He could not swallow. His niece, Mrs. Willis, said: "What is the matter, Uncle James?"

"Nothing more than a change of *mind*, my dear." His head . . . dropped, and he ceased breathing as quietly as the snuff of a candle goes out.[52]

Payne, afflicted by his loss, wrote a biographical note about his brother-in-law to send to John Quincy Adams, who would deliver a eulogy in Boston. He closed his note, writing: "He passed the bound of humanity without the slightest falter at its brink. Hero, Sage or Christian could have done no more." [53]

Hero. Some would vociferously deny that tribute to Madison. They would charge him with "the unforgivable sin" of our times, at least. He did *not* free his slaves (although he would so much have wanted to)—he did not go all the way with measures for complete and immediate emancipation.[54] Politely put, he is seen as resorting to half-measures in the great issue of equal human rights. No doubt. But can *we* say that even today Negro equality has reached its *full* measure? Will it come tomorrow, and by means of laws?

The "unforgivable sin" I should remind you changes with the time and situation. In Madison's entry on the scene of public affairs, to have failed to join the Revolution for Independence, to have failed to create a free and just design of government—would have been *the unforgivable sin.*

Are angry critics of the founding fathers themselves not chargeable with such commission? For is it not the unforgivable sin of critical intelligence to ask for all things at once and to narrow all human service to only one value and to only one insistent question? Blind to the great creativity and devotion that set us on the path of governing ourselves; ignorant of the relationships which half-measures bear to successive fuller measures, these critics are neither just nor wise.

There are *no* heroes. Men are not angels. But if "heroic" can properly be a human dimension, if greatness can apply to political man, then it does truly apply to Madison.

Thus, when John Quincy Adams spoke in Congress of Madison after his death, he asked: "Is it not in a pre-eminent degree by emanations from *his* mind, that we are assembled here as the representatives of the people and the states of this Union? Is it not transcendentally by his exertions that we address each other here by the endearing appellations of country-men and fellow-citizens?[55]

Madison's habitual candour and modesty would not have permitted him to accept as much.

But one thing he must have known to create that serenity so remarked on in his last years. William James once put it in a sentence: "The great use of a life is to spend it for something that outlasts it."

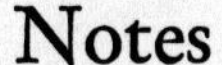

Notes

Notes

PREFACE

1. Paul Jennings, *A Colored Man's Reminiscences of James Madison* (Brooklyn, 1865), p. 19.

CHAPTER ONE

1. William T. Hutchinson and William M. E. Rachal, eds., *The Papers of James Madison* (Chicago, 1962), I, 43.

2. Original Draft in Madison's handwriting in the Madison Papers, Library of Congress. Also copy in the handwriting of Mrs. Madison may be found there. Until recently, it was assumed that Madison's "last message" was a dying injunction; and there was also considerable controversy beginning in the mid-nineteenth century, in the fevered climate of the Wilmot Proviso and the admission of California to the Union, over the authenticity of the message, as both secessionists and unionists hastened to claim the protection of Madison's mantle. The fact that the message was printed for the first time fourteen years after Madison's death, and in the context of the anti-slavery position invited exactly such alleged charges of spuriousness. It was Richard Rush who offered Madison's message to the public, and he had received it from Edward Coles eight years earlier. The whole affair is set to rights in Irving Brant's biography of James Madison, where he also includes a photograph of Madison's "Advice To My Country" in Madison's hand. See

Brant, *James Madison* (New York, 1961), VI (*Commander-in-Chief*), 530–31.

3. William Cabell Rives, *History of the Life and Times of James Madison* (Boston, 1859), I, 11.

4. This statement is taken from Madison's "Autobiography," an invaluable guide to the principal events and beliefs of the author's life, though very brief and called by him a mere "sketch" which he would have improved from its "crude" state had illness not prevented him. See his letter to J. K. Paulding, January ——, 1832, printed in Congress Edition, *Letters and Other Writings of James Madison* (Philadelphia, 1865), IV, 214. The "Autobiography" was relatively little known to historians until Douglass Adair, in 1945, printed it in the *William and Mary Quarterly*, taking the text from a manuscript copy in the Madison Papers at the Library of Congress. Adair argued persuasively in his introductory remarks that Madison was indeed the author of the short autobiographical sketch, although it was cast in the third person—a fact which one might attribute to the circumstance that Madison by 1832 was suffering from advanced arthritis in his hands, which made writing generally difficult for him, and which disposed him to dictate his correspondence to one or another of his relatives who could be found at Montpelier. It is clear from Adair's remarks (see his "James Madison's 'Autobiography,'" *William and Mary Quarterly*, Third Series, Vol. II, No. 2 [April 1945], 191–229) that Madison's authorship was still in question with historians and biographers. A personal letter to Adair from Irving Brant, Madison's most thorough biographer, indicated that Brant was not certain whether Madison could reliably and entirely be called the author of the sketch, although he conceded that it was likely.

After close comparison of the autobiographical document in the Madison Papers in the Library of Congress with one or two related documents, it is suggested a few modifications are necessary. It is now possible to state with increased assurance that Madison did dictate his "Autobiography," and that it is a trustworthy document of his own composition, even though it was dictated either to John C. Payne, his brother-in-law, or to Payne Todd, his stepson.

New light on the matter of authorship of the "Autobiography" is provided by the document (Ac. 2692, Madison Papers) which appears to have been prepared for John Quincy Adams, who had requested information about Madison (via a conversation with Mrs. Madison) in the summer of 1836, shortly after Madison's death, and prior to delivery of a eulogy of Madison in Congress on September 27, 1836. At first this document might be mistaken for an early draft of Madison's "Autobiography"—both Irving Brant and Douglass Adair so interpret it. But internal evidence indicates that although the writer used much of the material and phraseology in the "Autobiography," he must have done so by consulting a retained copy of the "Autobiography" or on the basis of notes he had written out for Madison as the latter dictated to him in 1831–32, prior to sending the sketch of his life to J. K. Paulding. In the "Autobiography," for example, Madison had paid a tribute to his beloved Dolley, commenting: "He [Madison] had also in the year 1794 entered the married state, with a partner who favoured these views, and added every happiness to his life which female merit could impart." In the later document, probably John C. Payne's, the writer prepared a biographical sketch of Madison for use by John Quincy Adams. The deleted clause referring to Dolley read: "and who, *he says*, added every happiness to his life which female merit could impart" (italics added). He carried the account of Madison's life only up to 1797, for beyond that period and to the close of Madison's political career, he judged that Mr. Adams' knowledge of public events and their actors would "need no light from other sources." But what is noteworthy is that the writer, referring to Mr. Madison's marriage in 1794, first copied Madison's tribute to Mrs. Madison and then on second thought, struck it out—though it is clearly legible in the manuscript. The enormous importance of the two little words "he says" is that they provide the testimony of John C. Payne, or another close relative, to Madison's own repeated references in his correspondence, to validate the fact that Madison was the author of the entire "Autobiography."

It is interesting to see the writer's comments upon the manner of Madison's death, remarks with which he brought to a close the informational sketch he was preparing for J. Q. Adams:

> In the later part of his [Madison's] life, chronic disease united the enfeebling effect of age to detract from its enjoyment & hasten its close. Tho' crippled in its use he long continued to employ his own pen, but when to this inconvenience was superadded a painful affection much increased by the necessary inclination of the chest in writing he resorted to dictation; and his compositions to the latest date . . . [missing word] till the hand of death was upon him, will bear scrutiny. As the purity of his life in retrospect casts no shadow to obscure the future he passed the bound of humanity with[out] the slightest falter at its brink. Hero, Sage or Christian could have done no more.

A document containing these precise remarks could hardly have *preceded*, or served as *the rough outline* for James Madison's "Autobiography."

5. Madison Papers, Library of Congress. Hutchinson and Rachal, *The Papers of James Madison*, I, publish only four extracts from Madison's "Notes on a brief system of logic," on the ground that "they lack originality both in organiza-

tion and thought" (I, 35). I cannot agree entirely with this judgment and its assumptions. A careful reading of Madison's "Notes on . . . logic" suggests that there is much more that is original than the editors allow, and in any case they are important because they reveal Madison's very early capacity, as a young college-age student, for philosophic analysis and the intellectual trait that remained with him throughout his life of independent scrutiny of supposedly "received" and "authoritative" opinion.

6. Adair, ed., "James Madison's 'Autobiography,' " pp. 198–99.

7. Madison to William Bradford, April 1, 1774, Hutchinson and Rachal, *The Papers of James Madison,* I, 112–13. For purposes of readability, I have spelled out abbreviated words in Madison's letters.

8. A detailed headnote on the Virginia Declaration of Rights, introducing the relevant documents, may be consulted in Hutchinson and Rachal, I, 170–79.

9. See John Locke, *A Letter Concerning Toleration.* For recent scholarship on the evaluation and circumstances of Locke's attempt to keep his authorship secret, see Maurice Cranston's careful biography, *John Locke* (New York, 1957).

10. Thomas Paine, *The Age of Reason.* Reprinted in H. H. Clark, *Thomas Paine: Representative Selections* (New York, 1944), 106.

11. Julian Boyd, ed., *The Papers of Thomas Jefferson* (Princeton, 1950, 17 vols. to date), I, 331. No student should miss the definitive discussion of the various stages of the drafting of the Virginia Constitution in Mr. Boyd's "Editorial Note," pp. 329–37.

12. The Madison quotation is from his letter to James Monroe, April 12, 1785, Gaillard Hunt, *The Writings of James Madison* (New York, 1900–10), II, 132. Madison added to his critical remarks on the Presbyterian clergy: "I

do not know a more shameful contrast than might be found between their memorials on the latter and former occasion."

The reference to those who favored "A Bill establishing a provision for Teachers of the Christian Religion" is in Hunt, *ibid.*, p. 183n. 1.

13. George Nicholas to Madison, April 22, 1785, *ibid.*, pp. 183–84n. 1.

14. George Nicholas to Madison, July 24, 1785, *ibid.*, p. 184n. 1; Madison to Jefferson, January 22, 1786, *ibid.*, p. 216. Also see Irving Brant, *James Madison*, II (*Nationalist*), p. 350.

15. Madison's *Memorial and Remonstrance Against Religious Assessments* is printed in Hunt, *The Writings of James Madison*, II, 183–91.

16. Madison to Jefferson, January 22, 1786, *ibid.*, p. 216. For the full text of Jefferson's "A Bill for Establishing Religious Freedom," including the enacting clauses, see Boyd, *The Papers of Thomas Jefferson*, II, 545–47. Also note Boyd's careful editorial analysis, *ibid.*, pp. 547–53.

17. This classic is in Jefferson's *Notes on the State of Virginia*, Query XVII. (William Peden's is the best current edition. Published for the Institute of Early American History and Culture at Williamsburg, Va., by the University of North Carolina Press [Chapel Hill, N.C., 1955], see p. 159.)

18. Mason's motion and the negative vote is reported in Hunt's edition of *The Journal of the Constitutional Convention*, *The Writings of James Madison*, IV, 442.

Madison's argument for ratification of the Constitution, bearing on this question, appears in several of his speeches at the Virginia Ratifying Convention. See Hunt, *The Writings of James Madison*, V, 136, 176, and 231. The sharpest statement occurs in his June 12, 1788 speech on religious freedom: "Is a bill of rights a security for religion? . . . If there were a majority of one sect, a bill of rights would be a poor protection for liberty. Happily for the States, they enjoy the utmost freedom of religion. This freedom arises from that multiplicity of sects, which pervades America, and which is the best and only security for religious liberty in any society. . . . There is not a shadow of right in the general government to intermeddle with religion. Its least interference with it, would be a most flagrant usurpation" (p. 176).

19. Jefferson to Madison, Paris, March 15, 1789, Boyd, *The Papers of Thomas Jefferson,* XIV, 659.

Madison manifestly came to accept this position by the time he introduced proposed amendments for a federal bill of rights in the First Congress. He said that the courts would "consider themselves in a peculiar manner the guardians of those rights; they would be an impenetrable bulwark against every assumption of power in the legislative or executive; they will be naturally led to resist every encroachment upon rights expressly stipulated for in the Constitution by the declaration of rights" (*Annals of the Congress of the United States,* I, 439).

It is of interest to note Jefferson's entire statement in this letter, vesting his hopes in judicial review for strengthening the proposed federal bill of rights. "This [the Judiciary] is a body, which if rendered independent and kept strictly to their own department, merits great confidence for their learning and integrity. In fact what degree of confidence would be too much for a body composed of such men as Wythe, Blair and Pendleton? On characters like these the "civiam ardor prova jubentium" would make no impression."

I have cited Jefferson's statement because it is little known and on the face of it contradicts his well known later opposition to the federal judiciary, particularly when he, as successful Republican President, was opposed by the Supreme Court under Chief Justice John Marshall. Perhaps the key to this zig-zag course on the role of the judiciary is Jefferson's view of its "independence." Jefferson did not believe that Marshall was anything but the Federalist partisan, using the powers of the Court to fight the Republican administration, and therefore not "independent." There is indeed strong evidence that outgoing President John Adams wanted the court to be a stronghold of Federalist party principles and therefore appointed John Marshall, knowing that he was an ardent enemy of Jefferson's, well-versed in the law, and young enough to expect that he would live through successive Republican administrations. See Page Smith's sympathetic biography of *John Adams* (New York, 1962), II, 1,063–64.

20. Hunt, *The Writings of James Madison,* V, 231–34; and Brant, *James Madison,* III (*Father of the Constitution*), pp. 225–28.

21. Hunt, *The Writings of James Madison,* V, 377.

22. *Ibid.*, pp. 378 and 387.

23. Adair, ed., "James Madison's Autobiography," p. 204.

24. Brant, *James Madison,* VI (*Commander-in-Chief*), 27–28.

25. *Ibid.*, p. 198.

26. Full text in Hunt, *The Writings of James Madison,* VIII, 132–33.

27. Hunt, *The Writings of James Madison,* IX, 126–27.

Madison was proud of having helped to found "an institution essentially unsectarian." He called this "the characteristic peculiarity of the University [of Virginia]." Letter to Chapman Johnson, May 8, 1828, Madison Papers, Library of Congress.

28. Madison's letter is printed in small type in Hunt, *The Writings of James Madison,* IX, 484–88. It is, however, mis-dated as "1832" and the recipient is identified only as "Rev. —— Adams." The letter does not appear in Hunt's index.

Notes

I came across this important letter in the Clements Library at the University of Michigan. The Rare Book Collection at Clements contains Jasper Adams' personal copy of his *Convention Sermon; on The Relation of Christianity to Civil Government in the United States of America* (Charleston, 1833). Adams' sermon was delivered in St. Michael's Church on February 13, 1833, before the Convention of the Protestant Episcopal Church of the Diocese of South Carolina.

The author's copy indicates that he sent his work to the men he considered most eminent in his day, with a note requesting from each recipient "a few lines expressive of his opinion of the validity of the argument herein contained." In this invaluable book, the author copied out in full the replies he had received from Madison, John Marshall, Joseph Story, J. S. Richardson, James Watson Williams, and in part a letter from Thomas Smith Grimké. At the conclusion of this series of faithfully copied letters is a list of over 200 men and learned societies or institutions who were also sent a copy of Adams' pamphlet. Among the men in this list are Andrew Jackson, Daniel Webster, Martin Van Buren, Edward Livingston, John C. Calhoun.

This unique volume permits us, first, to correct the date assigned to Madison's letter by Hunt, as well as in the Madison Papers in the Library of Congress, from 1832 to the spring of 1833. Second, it permits us to identify the recipient as the Reverend Jasper Adams, who was an outstanding educator. He had come from New England on grounds of health to take over the Presidency of Charleston College, and spent the last years of his life as a Professor of Moral Philosophy at the United States Military Academy.

The quotations in the text come from Jasper Adams' pamphlet in the Clements Library. In the case of the Madison letter, for convenience I have cited the text as given in Hunt's edition of Madison's writings.

29. As indicated in the previous note, Jasper Adams transcribed the replies in full from Chief Justice Marshall, dated May 9, 1833, and from Justice Story, dated May 14, 1833. Given the exactitude with which he copied Madison's letter, it is highly probable that these are exact copies of all the replies he received and transcribed. The quotations given in the text come from this source.

30. Justice Rutledge's dissenting opinion appears in *Everson v. Board of Education*, 330 U.S. 1 (1947). The quotations in the text may be found in the reprint published in Milton Konvitz, ed., *First Amendment Freedoms* (New York, 1961), pp. 18 and 20.

CHAPTER TWO

1. Interestingly enough, the reference to Madison as a little Applejohn is not necessarily a slight. As the Oxford Dictionary states, this variety of apple "is said to keep about two years and *is at perfection when it is shrivelled and withered*" (italics mine).

2. See Louis Hartz, *The Liberal Tradition in America* (New York, 1955).

3. Daniel Boorstin. The earlier position is developed in his *The Lost World of Thomas Jefferson* (New York, 1948). The later position is sketched in *The Genius of American Politics* (New York, 1953), and is maintained in *The Americans: The Colonial Experience* (New York, 1958). In *The Americans* the author wrote: "The appeal to self-evidence did not displace more academic and more dogmatic modes of thinking among all Americans, but American life nourished it until it became a prevailing mode. It was not the system of a few great American Thinkers, but the mood of Americans thinking. It rested on two sentiments. The first was a belief that the reasons men give for their positions are much less important than the

actions themselves, that it is better to act well for wrong or unknown reasons than to treasure a systematized 'truth' with ambiguous conclusions, that deep reflection does not necessarily produce the most effective system. The second was a belief that the novelties of experience must be freely admitted into men's thought. Why strain the New World through the philosophical sieves of the Old? If philosophy denied the innuendos of experience, the philosophy—not the experience—must be rejected. Therefore, a man's mind was wholesome not when it possessed the most refined implements for dissecting and ordering all knowledge, but when it was most sensitive to the unpredicted whisperings of environment. It was less important that the mind be elegantly furnished than that it be open and unencumbered" (pp. 151–52).

This far from clear passage sets up, by the author's recommended technique of "innuendos," a false dichotomy throughout, which does a disservice both to European and to American thought (and thinkers). A mind well furnished need not be "elegantly" (i.e., superficially, ostentatiously, merely fashionably) furnished. On the other hand, while Americans certainly did not need to "strain the New World through the philosophical sieves of the Old," why need they be held to "a philosophy of the unexpected" (p. 151)—whatever that is—and why should they be held to basing that philosophy on *sentiments* that made more of *actions* than it did of *reasons?*

4. Benjamin F. Wright (ed.), The *Federalist* by Alexander Hamilton, James Madison, and John Jay (Cambridge, Mass., 1961), Introduction, pp. 19–20.

5. Hunt, *The Writings of James Madison*, IX, 549.

6. Letter to William Cogswell, March 10, 1834, Hunt, *The Writings of James Madison*, IX, 533.

7. "Of Ancient and Modern Confederacies," in Hunt, *The Writings of James Madison*, II, 369–90. The editor's

footnote observes: "This memorandum is written on small sheets of paper, which, put together, formed a compact little book, suited to be carried in the pocket. There are 39 pages, and it would seem Madison intended extending it, for an extra page is headed 'Gryson Confederacy.'"

8. The editor, Fortunatio Bartolomeo de Felice (1723–89) was an Italian philosopher and mathematician, who himself was one of the panel of scholars and men of letters who contributed to the work, and who printed it on his own press in Yverdon in 1778.

9. Madison's "Observations" (April 1787) on the "Vices of the Political System of the U. States" is printed in Hunt, *The Writings of James Madison*, II, 361–69. This indispensable set of notes was destined to bear fruit in Madison's maturing political thought. He used these materials effectively in the debates; in the Constitutional Convention and gave them finely finished development in three interesting *Federalist* papers: Number 18, on the Greek Confederacies; Number 19, on certain medieval and modern confederacies; and Number 20 on the Netherlands Confederacy. It is unbelievable (but true) that historians and scholars continued, in the first sixty years of the twentieth century to contest that these papers were Madison's work, that they cared to offer a semblance of reasonable argument for Hamilton as their author, for the indubitable proof of Madison's authorship lay so easily to hand. His sketch of the vices of the ancient and modern confederacies, published in the 1901 Hunt edition of Madison's writings, should have cut the ground from any reasonable doubter. The historical data, the organization, features and flaws of the various confederacies, the flow of critical comment, the parallel phraseology and the entire drift of thought left no ground whatsoever for honest doubt. Yet these papers were commonly attributed to Hamilton and Madison as joint authors until Douglass Adair made a strong favorable case for Madison's

authorship in his excellent article, "The Authorship of the Disputed *Federalist* Papers," *William and Mary Quarterly*, Third Series, Vol. I, Nos. 2 and 3 (April and July 1944), 97–122, 235–64, especially pp. 104–105, 116–17, 249–50. Even after that there were Hamiltonian diehards and timorous historians who continued to attribute the papers to both men.

Some of these were finally instructed by the elaborate apparatus of the statistical study "Inference In An Authorship Problem: A Comparative Study of Discrimination Methods Applied to the Authorship of the *Federalist* papers," by Frederick Mosteller and David L. Wallace, a study presented as a paper at the statistical meetings in Minneapolis, September 9, 1962, and widely noticed in the American press thereafter. This study, as the newspaper headlines confidently disclosed, "settled" the matter. "Disputed Federalist Papers Are Laid to Madison" was the caption employed by the *New York Times*, September 10, 1962: subtitle "Computer Downgrades Role of Hamilton as Author of Several Essays." Actually, the study provides statistically high odds for Madison's authorship of the three papers (18, 19, 20) here under review, but its main conclusion concerns the twelve disputed papers, 49 to 58 and 62 to 63. The authors continue to refer to Numbers 18 to 20 as "joint papers" although they note the statistical edge in favor of Madison's authorship and promise "an investigation" of the writing of Number 20 (p. 12).

Actually, Madison's own statements about his and Hamilton's authorship have been so remarkably borne out by the scholarship referred to that his statement about these three so-called "joint" papers is perhaps the truest index of all. He stated that he had incorporated in them some little material gathered by Hamilton. In a note he made in his own copy of the *Federalist*, which is now in the Rare Book Division of the Library of Congress, Madison scrupulously acknowledged that a small part of the material for Numbers 18, 19, and 20 had been prepared by Alexander Hamilton.

Corroboration from the ranks of contemporary Hamiltonian scholars was provided by Broadus Mitchell in his biography of Alexander Hamilton (*Alexander Hamilton,* I (*Youth to Maturity, 1755–1788*) [New York, 1957]), where he judged these three papers to belong "to Madison (mostly)" (p. 420).

Sustaining Madison's claim to the authorship of Numbers 18, 19, and 20, Benjamin F. Wright, in his recent scholarly edition of the *Federalist,* attributed these papers to him. But the other major scholarly edition of the *Federalist* of recent vintage, by Jacob E. Cooke, formerly an assistant editor of *The Hamilton Papers,* attributes them to "James Madison (With the Assistance of Alexander Hamilton)." (Cooke, *The Federalist* [Middletown, Conn., 1961], pp. 110, 117, 124.) Thus the gap between contending scholarly champions has been virtually closed; the small crack that remains is entirely a matter of semantic preference, since Madison himself, while definitely asserting that he was the author of these papers, correctly acknowledged using some noted material of Hamilton's.

10. Madison here states succinctly the theme which was soon to be given classic foundation in his famous Tenth *Federalist* paper, concluding with this generalization: "The Society becomes broken into a greater variety of interests, of pursuits, of passions, which check each other, whilst those who may feel a common sentiment have less opportunity of communication and concert. It may be inferred that the inconvenience of popular States contrary to the prevailing Theory, are in proportion not to the extent, but to the narrowness of their limits" (p. 368).

11. An "Outline" of the relationship between state governments and the general government, showing the "awful consequences" of a final dissolution of the Union, Septem-

ber 1829, Hunt, *The Writings of James Madison*, IX, 351. Madison stated that it was a fundamental error to suppose the State Governments were parties to the Constitutional compact—the Constitution was created "by the people composing the respective States" (p. 352).

It is not clear whether Madison's "Outline" was intended to rehearse arguments for newspaper publication (to quell the rising tide of states' rights argument), or for a contemplated letter to an individual, who in turn might have been expected to give Madison's views wider circulation. The imprecatory style Madison employed lends support to the former hypothesis. The "Outline" concludes:

> The happy union of these States is a wonder; their Constitution a miracle; their example the hope of liberty throughout the world. Woe to the ambition that would meditate the destruction of either! (p. 357).

12. Patrick Henry, with deadly aim, spoofed the series of distinctions and negations by which Madison sought to suggest the radical newness of the American Federal system. He rose in the Virginia Ratifying Convention to dispose of Madison's arguments: "We may be amused if we please, by a treatise of political anatomy. In the brain it is national: the stamina are federal—some limbs are federal, others national. The senators are voted for by the state legislatures, so far it is federal. Individuals choose the members of the first branch; here it is national. It is federal in its conferring general powers; but national in retaining them. It is not to be supported by the states—the pockets of individuals are to be searched for its maintenance. What signifies it to me, that you have the most curious anatomical description of it in its creation. To all the common purpose of legislation, it is a great consolidation of government." (Jonathan Elliot, ed., *The Debates in the Several State Conventions on the Adoption of the Federal Constitution* [Washington,

D.C., 1836], II, 178–80.) Even in his late years, Madison counterposed to this type of argument his unruffled belief that "A Government like ours has so many safety-valves giving vent to overheated passions, that it carries within itself a relief against the infirmities from which the best of human Institutions cannot be exempt." (Letter to Lafayette, November 25, 1820, Hunt, *The Writings of James Madison*, IX, p. 36.) More pointedly, he consistently maintained that "those who deny the possibility of a political system, with a divided sovereignty like that of the U. S. must chuse between a government purely consolidated, & an association of Governments purely federal." (Madison's "Notes on Nullification," Hunt, *The Writings of James Madison*, IX, 605.)

13. Gaillard Hunt, "James Madison and Religious Liberty," *American Historical Association Report*, 1901, I, 170.

14. Wright, ed., *The Federalist*, p. 355. This and subsequent quotations in this chapter from *The Federalist* are from the text in Wright's 1961 edition.

15. *Ibid.*, p. 356.

16. *Ibid.*

17. *Ibid.*

18. *Ibid.*, p. 357.

19. *Ibid.*, p. 358.

20. *Ibid.*

21. *Ibid.*, p. 359.

22. Alpheus T. Mason, "The *Federalist*—A Split Personality," *American Historical Review*, LVII, No. 3 (April 1952), 625–43. See also a discussion of Madison's political outlook in A. Koch, *Power, Morals, and the Founding Fathers* (Ithaca, N.Y., 1961), 106–21, where comparison with Hamilton's is made.

23. *Ibid.*, pp. 50–60.

24. Brant, *James Madison*, VI (*Commander-in-Chief*), 528.

25. James Barbour, *Eulogium Upon the Life and Character of James Madison* (Printed by Gales and Seaton, Washington, D.C., 1836).

26. *Ibid.*, p. 16.

27. Senator Robbins advocated the passage of the Senate resolution to purchase the Madison manuscripts from Mrs. Madison, with a supporting speech from which the excerpts cited above constitute a small part. The speech is printed in full in the Introduction to Henry D. Gilpin's edition of *The Papers of James Madison* (Washington, D.C., 1840) I, xviii–xxiv.

28. Nelson A. Rockefeller, *The Future of Federalism* (Cambridge, Mass., 1962), pp. 27–28.

CHAPTER THREE

1. January 20, 1827, Madison Papers, Library of Congress.

2. See footnote 2, Chapter One.

3. Letter to Sparks, June 1, 1831, Hunt, *The Writings of James Madison*, IX, 460.

4. Mary Cutts' manuscript memoir of Dolley Madison (1855?), microfilm, Library of Congress.

5. *Ibid.*

6. *An Address Delivered Before the Agricultural Society of Albemarle*, on Tuesday, May 12, 1818, by Mr. Madison, President of the Society. Richmond, Shepherd, and Pollard, 1818, 15–16. The vigor and philosophical approach in this unlikely-sounding *Address* of Madison's must, I suppose, be read to be believed. Suffice it to say that he chides Virginians for failing to make the progressive innovations in agriculture that make human well-being more secure, pointing out that the "actual sufferings from a deficient and precarious subsistence" characterize the savage,

as different from the civilized life, and that an aversion to change is pitiable in the uncivilized, contemptible in the civilized. Warning of the ease with which civilized people "slide" into the ways of the savage, Madison pokes fun at the myth of the "return to the pristine life." Writing as a true man of the Enlightenment, Madison points out the intimate connection between agricultural progress and knowledge of the implements and resources. No more than with manufactures nor trade is the "process of opening and stirring the soil . . . an easy operation." Man's "effort and contrivance," however much human inclination yearns for ease and the pristine life, are the price of plenty and civilization. The first settlers in this country knew this, made their choice, and decisively shaped history in a direction that taught the value of arts beyond their *immediate wants.* They *could have* "degenerated into savage tribes."

7. Recorded in a memoir of a four-day visit and extensive conversation with Madison by Jesse B. Harrison that took place at Montpelier, November 27 to 30, 1827. In the J. B. Harrison Papers, Library of Congress.

8. Letter to Professor James A. G. Davis, 1832, The Congress Edition, *Letters and Writings of James Madison* (Philadelphia, 1865), IV, 259. This lengthy and substantial letter to James A. G. Davis, who was a young professor of law at the University of Virginia, is marked "not sent." The editor of the Congress Edition put the substitute suggested date of "1833" in square brackets after the earlier date which the letter bore. The letter runs to roughly twelve thousand words and is really a political essay on Madison's views of the constitutional power of Congress to promote and protect domestic manufacturing. Davis had sent him a copy of some lectures in which he had taken issue with Madison on this subject. Madison, in rejecting the sectional argument that the tariff for the encouragement of manufactures was unconstitutional, stated that he was

aware that his views were "in opposition to the dominant opinions in Virginia as well as elsewhere." He was equally aware, he said, that "the high degree of excitement in which these opinions are involved," was unwilling to heed reasoning. He hoped those passions would calm down and men would cease, in time, to attribute "all sufferings, public and private, real and imaginary" to the tariff "as the sole cause of them." He made short shrift of the argument that the Northern manufacturing interests had created the tariff as "a system of plunder, wresting the money from the pockets of the Southern agriculturalist and putting it into the pockets of the Northern manufacturers" (p. 260). Instead, he pointed realistically to the *diversified* economy of the North and attributed the economic depression in the South to the decline of land values and the falling prices for her great staple exports. He concluded that as the Southern section becomes manufacturing, diversifying its previous exclusive employment of labor in agriculture, differences between North and South would be reduced—"and with it the conflicting views engendered by it" (p. 264).

9. Julian Boyd, *Number 7: Alexander Hamilton's Secret Attempts to Control American Foreign Policy* (Princeton, 1964). In this pathbreaking study of Hamilton's activities as "Number 7" (so he was designated in the dispatches of a British secret agent) to establish a closer connection with Great Britain than official American foreign policy intended in 1790, Mr. Boyd concludes, on the basis of the record and careful scrutiny, that Hamilton deliberately employed deception in his relations with President Washington on questions of great public importance. My review of Boyd's *Number 7* appeared in *The American Scholar*, Vol. 23, No. 2 (Spring 1965), 306–11.

10. See Chapter 7 in Koch, *Jefferson and Madison, The Great Collaboration* (New York, 1950), pp. 174–211.

11. Madison's "Report on the Resolutions of 1798" is

printed in Hunt, *The Writings of James Madison*, VI, 341–406. Madison had expressly re-entered the House of Delegates in order to review the replies of the various states on the Virginia Resolutions, and to review the meaning of the Alien and Sedition Laws.

12. *Ibid.*, p. 397.

13. *Ibid.*, p. 398.

14. *Ibid.*, p. 405.

15. *Ibid.*, p. 406.

16. Hunt, *The Writings of James Madison*, IX, 383–96. Madison's draft was dated "Apr. (say 3d or 4th)." Hunt printed this immensely important letter as footnote material on the pages cited, even though three-fourths of each page had to be allotted to it.

17. *Ibid.*, p. 385n.

18. *Ibid.*, p. 389n.

19. Madison to Everett, September 10, 1830, Congress Edition, *Writings*, IV, 109–110.

20. Madison to Hayne, *ibid.*, p. 387n.

21. Madison to General Lafayette, December 12, 1830, Madison Papers, Library of Congress. Madison concedes that a constitutional monarchy may be necessary to the actual condition of France and that as an expedient, it might be easier "to descend to a more popular form, than to control the tendency of a premature experiment to confusion, and its usual result in arbitrary government." He comments of himself, "Republican as I am" and goes on to urge a "federal mixture" which he asserts will improve any Republic. He concludes with a statement of his ultimate political belief: "In the contingency of a practical question of a Government involving the element of Federalism, every light reflected from our experiment may have a degree of interest." The letter throughout is an admirable blend of personal affection, diffidence in pressing his views upon a man in the midst of his own political decisions, and unshakable

conviction that a federal republic on the lines of the American Experiment is relevant to every country that seeks to advance in political liberty. The July Revolution ("the three glorious days of July") provided the context for Madison's remarks to his good old friend.

22. Madison's memo in which he suggests the worldwide potential application of the federal principle is cited in Brant, *James Madison,* VI (*Commander-in-Chief*), 529–30. It is in the Madison Papers, Library of Congress, Volume 90. A few items earlier there is another memorandum on a scrap of paper in which Madison expressed a cognate thought. "All governments hitherto bad," he wrote, "either tending to despotism or to anarchy and through that to despotism. The expedient of federal republic, aiming at a security against both, merits a fair experiment and the good wishes of all. It has controlled the general government through the states, as in Alien and Sedition laws, and the states when flying individually out of their orbits have under the influence of the government and the frowns of other states returned into their regular paths—so Massachusetts, Kentucky, Georgia and—so it is hoped will South Carolina. The wrong get right before the right get wrong. The silent control of the general government has a great preventive effect, in the absence of which individual states might go wrong without otherwise being aware of the propensity to do so." The memo was probably composed late in 1828 or 1829, with the exception of the phrase concerning his hope for South Carolina, which was written later. The focus in this memo is principally on the federal system of the United States, to be sure; but the general virtues of the system, correcting the "hitherto bad" governments under which humanity had suffered, had nothing to do with geographical boundary lines.

23. Madison to Andrew Stevenson, February 10, 1833, Congress Edition, *Writings*, IV, 272–73.

24. Madison to Richard Rush, March 15, 1831, Madison Papers, Library of Congress.

25. Harriet Martineau, *Retrospect of Western Travel* (London and New York, 1838), pp. 190–91. The whole chapter "Madison" (189–98) is an invaluable record of Madison's conversation and behavior in February of 1834, and in any case too good to miss.

26. Madison to Randolph, July 26, 1785, Hunt, *The Writings of James Madison*, II, 154.

27. An informative study is Beverley B. Munford, *Virginia's Attitude Toward Slavery and Secession* (Richmond, Va., 1909), despite the author's avowed purpose of justifying the moral and legal position that led to Virginia's secession in the Civil War. Although a recent study, Robert McColley, *Slavery and Jeffersonian Virginia* (Urbana, Ill., 1964), fails even to mention this pre-World War I study in the bibliographical note, the neglect is undeserved—and appears to be explicable only in terms of ignorance or idealogical bias. Typical of McColley's disingenuous analysis is the following statement: "Only George Wythe, among all the eminent thinkers of Jeffersonian Virginia, was willing to reason from the fundamental principle of the Negro's rights as a human being, and to allow the claims of planters to suffer if they must. The assaults on slavery by all the other renowned intellects of Virginia were, by contrast to the positions of the mildest abolitionists, practical endorsements of the status quo" (pp. 35–36). It is not clear whether McColley means: (1) that Jefferson, Madison, and other "renowned intellects" of Virginia were unwilling to *reason* from the principle of the Negro's rights as a human being; or (2) that they were willing to so reason but unwilling to "allow the claims of planters to suffer if they must"; or (3) that they were unwilling to so reason *and also* unwilling to allow the claims of planters to suffer; or (4) that they were both willing to so reason and willing to

allow the claims of planters to suffer if they must, but that nonetheless by contrast to "the mildest abolitionists" their positions were "practical endorsements of the status quo." There can be no doubt that if (1) is meant, it is simply false. Then the Virginians must at least be credited with creditable *verbal* positions! If (2) is meant, only those who believe in a single absolute value can dismiss out of hand "the *claims*" of a group of men without considering whether they are just claims or whether there are alternative ways and means to recognize the claims, if just, and alleviate the suffering, if humanly possible. In short, (2) implies an absolute good and evil, an absolute right and wrong—without scrutiny of the *conflicting goods and evils*, the *conflicting rights and wrongs*, and the reasonable ways to attempt to avoid the greater evil and act in accord with the lesser evil. If (3) is meant, it is vitiated by the falsity of (1) and the dogmatic oversimplification of the problem as formulated in (2). If (4) is meant—that the Virginians both condemned slavery out of moral regard for the human rights of the Negro and were willing to allow the claims of the planter to suffer if they must, but that they failed to measure up to "the mildest abolitionist" and thus their positions were "practical endorsements of the status quo"—in short, they were virtually advocates of slavery, *no matter what they said*, and *no matter what means they were using or prepared to use to bring slavery into an eventual decline and extinction*, because they did not call, as even the *mildest* abolitionist did, for "*immediate and unconditional*" abolition of slavery. These statements would not be worth this perfunctory analysis if it were not for the fact that they are similar to others on almost every page of a study that purports to be an "objective" work of modern "scholarship."

28. Madison to James Madison [Senior]. Hunt, *The Writings of James Madison*, II, 15.

29. Charles C. Tansill, *Documents Illustrative of the Formation of the Union of the American States* (House Document No. 398, Government Printing Office, Washington, D.C., 1927), p. 618. (Madison's Notes of the Debates in the Constitutional Convention, dateline Saturday, August 25, 1787). Madison's protest against the odious slave trade was backed up by his vote against the measure to legalize it for the period from 1787 to 1808. The lineup *for* the measure was New Hampshire, Massachusetts, Connecticut, Maryland, North Carolina, South Carolina, and Georgia. *Against* the measure were New Jersey, Pennsylvania, Delaware, and Virginia.

In the First Congress, in April 1789, Madison supported Josiah Parker and Theodoric Bland—all three Virginians seeking to amend the tariff bill then under discussion by a clause levying an import tax of ten dollars upon every slave brought into the country. Madison stated: "The clause in the constitution allowing a tax to be imposed though the traffic could not be prohibited for twenty years, was inserted, he believed, for the very purpose of enabling Congress to give some testimony of the sense of America with respect to the African trade.

By expressing a national disapprobation of that trade it is to be hoped we may destroy it, and so save ourselves from reproaches and our posterity from the imbecility ever attendant on a country filled with slaves." (*Annals of Congress*, Vol. I, April 15, 24, 1789.)

30. Wright, ed., *The Federalist*, p. 278.

31. *Ibid.*, p. 304.

32. Jefferson's Sixth Annual Message, December 2, 1806, Paul Leicester Ford, *The Writings of Thomas Jefferson* (New York, 1897), VIII, 492–93.

33. Madison's Second Annual Message, December 5, 1810, Hunt, *The Writings of James Madison*, VIII, 127–28.

34. Madison's Eighth Annual Message, December 3, 1816, *ibid.*, p. 380.

35. Brant, *James Madison*, V (*President*), pp. 224–25.

36. Madison to Robert J. Evans, June 15, 1819, Hunt, *The Writings of James Madison*, VIII, 440. This entire letter deserves scrutiny from anyone who wishes to understand Madison's position on general emancipation as an end, and on a careful and equitable policy of compensation and colonization as means. Whatever else it shows, it conclusively proves that he was earnestly searching for a workable plan of general emancipation even before the Missouri Compromise, and that he believed that the creation of a satisfactory remedy for this, as for other "deeprooted and wide-spread evils," would depend upon the recognition that it should be gradual. See *ibid.*, pp. 439–47, for this important document.

37. Responding to the invitation to become President, transmitted to him by the Secretary of the Society, Reverend R. R. Gurley, Madison wrote (February 19, 1833): I have received your letter . . . informing me that I have been unanimously elected to the office of President by the "American Colonization Society."

The great and growing importance of the Society and the signal philanthropy of its members give to the distinction conferred on me a value of which I am deeply sensible.

It is incumbent on me, at the same time, to say, that my very advanced age and impaired health leave me no hope of an adequacy to the duties of the station which I should be proud to perform. It will not the less be my earnest prayer that every success may reward the labours of an Institution which, though so humble in its origin, is so noble in its object of removing a great evil from its own country by means which may communicate to another the greatest of blessings.

Congress Edition, *Writings*, IV, 274.

38. Madison to Thomas R. Dew, February 23, 1833, Hunt, *The Writings of James Madison*, IX, 498–502.

39. Madison's belief that it was the obligation of both state and national government to support whatever expenses were incurred in effecting a safe, orderly, and effective program for gradual emancipation was stated on innumerable occasions. For a typical expression of his position, see the letter to Dew cited above, or the letter already cited to Robert J. Evans. (Hunt, VIII, 439–47.)

40. Coles' Autobiographical statement, January 7, 1847, to J. M. Peck, and cited by Peck in letter to H. Warren, March 26, 1855, Clarence Walworth Alvord, ed., *Collections of the Illinois Historical Library,* Vol. XV: Biographical Series, Vol. I (*Governor Edward Coles*). (Springfield, Ill., 1920), Appendix, p. 330.

41. After a record that made some progressive improvements with respect to slavery in the period after the Revolution, Virginia enacted reactionary statutes in 1806 and subsequently, providing that freed Negroes must depart from the state within twelve months after manumission. Munford, *Virginia's Attitude Toward Slavery and Secession,* pp. 42–43.

42. E. B. Washburne, *Sketch of Edward Coles* (Chicago, 1882), pp. 43–46. This biographical sketch is reprinted in the volume edited by Alvord (see note 40 above).

43. Alvord, *op. cit.,* unnumbered page preceding *Washburne's Governor Edward Coles.*

44. [L. B. Cutts], *Memoirs and Letters of Dolley Madison,* Edited by Her Grand-Niece (Boston, 1886), pp. 5–9.

45. Madison to Edward Coles, October 19, 1822, Madison Papers, Library of Congress.

46. Madison to Edward Coles, August 29, 1834, Hunt, *The Writings of James Madison,* IX, 540.

47. Edward Coles to Jefferson, July 31, 1814, Alvord, *op. cit.,* p. 23. Jefferson's letter replying to Coles (*ibid.,* pp.

24–27) and Coles' response to it (*ibid.*, pp. 28–30), pursue the subject and constitute a noteworthy exchange of emotionally charged ideas.

48. Jefferson to Coles, August 25, 1814. This is the letter cited above (Alvord, pp. 24–27). It is both printed in full and a facsimile copy in Jefferson's handwriting is tipped in between pp. 24–25 of this volume.

49. Cited in Brant, *James Madison,* VI (*Commander-in-Chief*), 518.

50. *Ibid.*, p. 519.

51. Madison's letter to Tucker suggests a coda to the recurrent themes of his life. That his last dictated discourse should be concerned with the mention and memory of his greatest friend, Jefferson, is in itself eloquent. But Madison made a specific connection between their two lives, telling Tucker of his satisfaction with the study of Jefferson "with whose principles of liberty and political career mine have been so extensively congenial." He mentioned Tucker's feeling of personal friendship that prompted the great credit he allowed to Madison's public services, and said that he had habitually justified his own deficiencies by his consciousness of "an ardent zeal . . . in promoting such a reconstruction of our political system as would provide for the permanent liberty and happiness of the United States."

His closing salutation took cognizance of the fact that every arduous struggle, in art and knowledge as in life, comes within sight of the end, congratulating Tucker "on the near approach to the end of your undertaking." Congress Edition, *Writings*, IV, 435–36.

52. Jennings, *ibid.*, p. 20.

53. This valuable document, a rough draft probably in the handwriting of John C. Payne, must have been prepared on or just before July 30, 1836. It embodies much of the language and information of Madison's "Autobiography" (see note 4, Chapter One), but the comment

above and other comments throughout the memorandum could not possibly have been dictated by Madison. I do not believe this document has ever been printed or made use of in the literature on Madison. Madison Papers, Library of Congress.

54. Financial embarrassment, in some part attendant upon the heavy expenses of covering for his profligate stepson, John Payne Todd, interfered with his long-nourished plan to free his slaves. (See Brant, *James Madison*, VI [*Commander-in-Chief*], 510–11.) Madison in the course of two decades of economic depression had spent $40,000 on Dolley Madison's spendthrift son. Edward Coles testified to the fact that Madison's intention was to include an emancipation provision in his will. Instead, Madison was forced to sell land and, worried about his wife's future, provided in his will that she should have the proceeds from the sale of his manuscripts. Under these circumstances the bequest he made to the American Colonization Society of two thousand dollars, out of the fund he anticipated from the proceeds of sale of his notes on the Constitutional Convention, is of marked interest. Hunt, *The Writings of James Madison*, IX, 550.

55. John Quincy Adams' speech in the House of Representatives on June 30, 1836, is printed in the Introduction to Henry D. Gilpin, ed., *Papers of Madison*, pp. viii–x. The quoted statement appears on p. ix.

Bibliographical List

Bibliographical List

Adair, Douglass. "James Madison's 'Autobiography,'" *William and Mary Quarterly*, Third Series, Vol. II, No. 2 (April 1945).

Alvord, Clarence Walworth, ed. *Collections of the Illinois Historical Library.* Springfield, Ill., 1920.

Annals of the Congress. Debates and Proceedings in the Congress of the United States, 1789–1824. 42 vols. Washington, 1834–56.

Barbour, James. *Eulogium Upon the Life and Character of James Madison.* Washington, D.C., 1836.

Boorstin, Daniel. *The Lost World of Thomas Jefferson.* New York, 1948.

———. *The Genius of American Politics.* New York, 1953.

———. *The Americans: The Colonial Experience.* New York, 1957.

Boyd, Julian, ed. *The Papers of Thomas Jefferson.* 17 vols. to date. Princeton, 1950.

Boyd, Julian. *Number 7: Alexander Hamilton's Secret Attempts to Control American Foreign Policy.* Princeton, 1964.

Brant, Irving. *James Madison.* New York, 1961.

Cooke, Jacob E., ed. *The Federalist.* Middletown, Conn., 1961.

Cranston, Maurice. *John Locke.* New York, 1957.

Bibliographical List

[Cutts, L. B.]. *Memoirs and Letters of Dolley Madison.* Edited by her Grand-niece. Boston, 1886.

Cutts, Mary. Manuscript memoir of Dolley Madison (1855?). Microfilm, Library of Congress.

Elliot, Jonathan, ed. *The Debates in the Several State Conventions on the Adoption of the Federal Constitution.* Washington, D.C., 1836.

Ford, Paul Leicester, ed. *The Writings of Thomas Jefferson.* 10 vols. New York, 1892–99.

Gilpin, Henry D., ed. *The Papers of James Madison.* Washington, D.C., 1840.

Harrison, J. B. Papers. Library of Congress.

Hartz, Louis. *The Liberal Tradition in America.* New York, 1955.

Hunt, Gaillard. *The Writings of James Madison.* New York, 1900–10.

———. "James Madison and Religious Liberty," *American Historical Association Report*, 1901, I, 170.

Hutchinson, William T. and William M. E. Rachal, eds. *The Papers of James Madison*, 4 vols. to date. Chicago, 1962.

Jennings, Paul. *A Colored Man's Reminiscences of James Madison.* Brooklyn, 1865.

Koch, Adrienne. *Jefferson and Madison: The Great Collaboration.* New York, 1950.

———. *Power, Morals, and the Founding Fathers.* Ithaca, N.Y., 1961.

Konvitz, Milton, ed. *First Amendment Freedoms: Selected Cases on Freedom of Religion, Speech, Press, Assembly.* New York, 1961.

McColley, Robert. *Slavery and Jeffersonian Virginia.* Urbana, Ill., 1964.

[Madison]. *Letters and Other Writings of James Madison.* Congress Edition, 4 vols. Philadelphia, 1865.

Madison Papers. Library of Congress.

Martineau, Harriet. *Retrospect of Western Travel.* London and New York, 1838.

Mason, Alpheus T. "The *Federalist*—A Split Personality," *American Historical Review*, LVII, No. 3 (April 1952).

Mitchell, Broadus. *Alexander Hamilton.* New York, 1957.

Mosteller, Frederick and David L. Wallace. "Inference In An Authorship Problem: A Comparative Study of Discrimination Methods Applied to the Authorship of the *Federalist* Papers," study presented as a paper at the statistical meetings in Minneapolis, September 9, 1962.

Munford, Beverley B. *Virginia's Attitude Toward Slavery and Secession.* Richmond, Va., 1909.

Paine, Thomas. *The Age of Reason.* Reprinted in H. H. Clark, ed., *Thomas Paine: Representative Selections.* New York, 1944.

Peden, William, ed. Jefferson's *Notes on the State of Virginia.* Published for the Institute of Early American History and Culture at Williamsburg, Va., by the University of North Carolina Press, Chapel Hill, N.C., 1955.

Richmond, ed. *An Address Delivered Before the Agricultural Society of Albemarle,* on Tuesday, May 12, 1818, by Mr. Madison, President of the Society (1818).

Rives, William Cabell. *History of the Life and Times of James Madison.* 3 vols. Boston, 1859–68.

Rockefeller, Nelson A. *The Future of Federalism.* Cambridge, Mass., 1962.

Smith, Page. *John Adams.* New York, 1962.

Tansill, Charles C. *Documents Illustrative of the Formation of the Union of the American States.* House Document No. 398, Government Printing Office, Washington, D.C., 1927.

Washburne, E. B. *Sketch of Edward Coles.* Chicago, 1882.

Wright, Benjamin F., ed. The *Federalist*, by Alexander Hamilton, James Madison, and John Jay. Cambridge, Mass. (The John Harvard Library), 1961.

Index

Index

Index

Index

Index

Index

Index

Index

Index

Index

Index

Index